THE COMPLETE BOOK OF
SLOW COOKING

pil

Publications International, Ltd.

Pictured on the front cover: Andouille and Cabbage *(page 154)*.
Pictured on the back cover *(clockwise from top left):* Cod Fish Stew *(page 113)*, Three-Bean Chili with Chorizo *(page 102)*, Shredded Beef Fajitas *(page 166)*, Lamb and Chickpea Stew *(page 122)*, Mixed Berry Cobbler *(page 302)* and Black Bean, Zucchini and Corn Enchiladas *(page 246)*.

ISBN: 978-1-68022-865-6

Library of Congress Control Number: 2017931279

Manufactured in China.

8 7 6 5 4 3 2 1

TABLE OF CONTENTS

SLOW COOKING TIPS

SIZES OF CROCK-POT® SLOW COOKERS

Smaller **CROCK-POT®** slow cookers—such as 1- to 3½-quart models—are the perfect size for cooking for singles, a couple, or empty nesters (and also for serving dips).

While medium-size **CROCK-POT®** slow cookers (those holding somewhere between 3 quarts and 5 quarts) will easily cook enough food at one time to feed a small family, they are also convenient for holiday side dishes or appetizers.

Large **CROCK-POT®** slow cookers are great for large family dinners, holiday entertaining, and potluck suppers. A 6- to 7-quart model is ideal if you like to make meals in advance. Or, have dinner tonight and store leftovers for later.

TYPES OF CROCK-POT® SLOW COOKERS

Current **CROCK-POT®** slow cookers come equipped with many different features and benefits, from auto-cook programs to oven-safe stoneware to timed programming. Please visit **WWW.CROCK-POT.COM** to find the **CROCK-POT®** slow cooker that best suits your needs.

How you plan to use a **CROCK-POT®** slow cooker may affect the model you choose to purchase. For everyday cooking, choose a size large enough to serve your family. If you plan to use the **CROCK-POT®** slow cooker primarily for entertaining, choose one of the larger sizes. Basic **CROCK-POT®** slow cookers can hold as little as 16 ounces or as much as 7 quarts. The smallest sizes are great for keeping dips warm on a buffet, while the larger sizes can more readily fit large quantities of food and larger roasts.

COOKING, STIRRING, AND FOOD SAFETY

CROCK-POT® slow cookers are safe to leave unattended. The outer heating base may get hot as it cooks, but it should not pose a fire hazard. The heating element in the heating base functions at a low wattage and is safe for your countertops.

Your **CROCK-POT®** slow cooker should be filled about one-half to three-fourths full for most recipes unless otherwise instructed. Lean meats such as chicken or pork tenderloin will cook faster than meats with more connective tissue and fat such as beef chuck or pork shoulder. Bone-in meats will take longer than boneless cuts. Typical **CROCK-POT®** slow cooker dishes take approximately 7 to 8 hours to reach the simmer point on LOW and about 3 to 4 hours on HIGH. Once the vegetables and meat start to simmer and braise, their flavors will fully blend and meat will become fall-off-the-bone tender.

According to the U.S. Department of Agriculture, all bacteria are killed at a temperature of 165°F. It's important to follow the recommended cooking times and not to open the lid often, especially early in the cooking process when heat is building up inside the unit. If you need to open the lid to check on your food or add additional ingredients, remember to allow additional cooking time if necessary to ensure food is cooked through and tender.

Large **CROCK-POT®** slow cookers, the 6- to 7-quart sizes, may benefit from a quick stir halfway through cook time to help distribute heat and promote even cooking. It's usually unnecessary to stir at all, as even ½ cup liquid will help to distribute heat and the stoneware is the perfect medium for holding food at an even temperature throughout the cooking process.

OVEN-SAFE STONEWARE

All **CROCK-POT®** slow cooker removable stoneware inserts may (without their lids) be used safely in ovens at up to 400°F. In addition, all **CROCK-POT®** slow cookers are microwavable without their lids. If you own another slow cooker brand, please refer to your owner's manual for specific stoneware cooking medium tolerances.

FROZEN FOOD

Frozen food can be successfully cooked in a **CROCK-POT®** slow cooker. However, it will require longer cooking time than the same recipe made with fresh food. Using an instant-read thermometer is recommended to ensure meat is fully cooked.

PASTA AND RICE

If you are converting a recipe for your **CROCK-POT®** slow cooker that calls for uncooked pasta, first cook the pasta on the stovetop just until slightly tender. Then add the pasta to the **CROCK-POT®** slow cooker. If you are converting a recipe for the

CROCK-POT® slow cooker that calls for cooked rice, stir in raw rice with the other recipe ingredients plus ¼ cup extra liquid per ¼ cup of raw rice.

BEANS

Beans must be softened completely before combining with sugar and/or acidic foods in the **CROCK-POT®** slow cooker. Sugar and acid have a hardening effect on beans and will prevent softening. Fully cooked canned beans may be used as a substitute for dried beans.

VEGETABLES

Root vegetables often cook more slowly than meat. Cut vegetables accordingly to cook at the same rate as meat—large or small or lean versus marbled—and place near the sides or bottom of the stoneware to facilitate cooking.

HERBS

Fresh herbs add flavor and color when added at the end of the cooking cycle; if added at the beginning, many fresh herbs' flavor will dissipate over long cook times. Ground and/or dried herbs and spices work well in slow cooking and may be added at the beginning of cook time. For dishes with shorter cook times, hearty fresh herbs such as rosemary and thyme hold up well. The flavor power of all herbs and spices can vary greatly depending on their particular strength and shelf life. Use chili powders and garlic powder sparingly, as these can sometimes intensify over the long cook times. Always taste the finished dish and correct seasonings including salt and pepper.

LIQUIDS

It's not necessary to use more than ½ to 1 cup liquid in most instances since juices in meats and vegetables are retained more in slow cooking than in conventional cooking. Excess liquid can be cooked down and concentrated after slow cooking on the stovetop or by removing meat and vegetables from the stoneware, stirring in one of the following thickeners and setting the **CROCK-POT®** slow cooker to HIGH. Cover; cook on HIGH for approximately 15 minutes or until juices are thickened.

FLOUR: All-purpose flour is often used to thicken soups or stews. Stir water into the flour in a small bowl until smooth. With the **CROCK-POT®** slow cooker on HIGH, whisk flour mixture into the liquid in the **CROCK-POT**® slow cooker. Cover; cook on HIGH 15 minutes or until the mixture is thickened.

CORNSTARCH: Cornstarch gives sauces a clear, shiny appearance; it's used most often for sweet dessert sauces and stir-fry sauces. Stir water into the cornstarch in a small bowl until the cornstarch is dissolved. Quickly stir this mixture into the liquid in the **CROCK-POT**® slow cooker; the sauce will thicken as soon as the liquid simmers. Cornstarch breaks down with too much heat, so never add it at the beginning of the slow cooking process and turn off the heat as soon as the sauce thickens.

TAPIOCA: Tapioca is a starchy substance extracted from the root of the cassava plant. Its greatest advantage is that it withstands long cooking, making it an ideal choice for slow cooking. Add tapioca at the beginning of cooking and you'll get a clear, thickened sauce in the finished dish. Dishes using tapioca as a thickener are best cooked on the LOW setting; it may become stringy when boiled for a long time.

MILK

Milk, cream, and sour cream break down during extended cooking. When possible, add them during the last 15 to 30 minutes of slow cooking, until just heated through. Condensed soups may be substituted for milk and may cook for extended times.

FISH

Fish is delicate and should be stirred into the **CROCK-POT**® slow cooker gently during the last 15 to 30 minutes of cooking. Cover; cook just until cooked through and serve immediately.

BAKED GOODS

If you wish to prepare bread, cakes, or pudding cakes in a **CROCK-POT**® slow cooker, you may want to purchase a covered, vented metal cake pan accessory for your **CROCK-POT**® slow cooker. You can also use any straight-sided soufflé dish or deep cake pan that will fit into the stoneware of your unit. Baked goods can be prepared directly in the stoneware; however, they can be a little difficult to remove from the insert, so follow the recipe directions carefully.

BREAKFAST AND BRUNCH

OVERNIGHT BREAKFAST PORRIDGE

Makes 4 servings

¾ cup steel-cut oats

¼ cup uncooked quinoa, rinsed and drained

¼ cup dried cranberries, plus additional for serving

¼ cup raisins

3 tablespoons ground flax seeds

2 tablespoons chia seeds

¼ teaspoon ground cinnamon

2½ cups almond milk, plus additional for serving

Maple syrup (optional)

¼ cup sliced almonds, toasted*

To toast almonds, spread in single layer in heavy skillet. Cook over medium heat 1 to 2 minutes or until nuts are lightly browned, stirring frequently.

1. Combine oats, quinoa, ¼ cup cranberries, raisins, flax seeds, chia seeds and cinnamon in heat-safe bowl that fits inside of 5- or 6-quart **CROCK-POT**® slow cooker. Stir in 2½ cups almond milk.

2. Place bowl into **CROCK-POT**® slow cooker; pour enough water to come halfway up side of bowl.

3. Cover; cook on LOW 8 hours. Carefully remove bowl from **CROCK-POT**® slow cooker. Stir in additional almond milk. Top with syrup, almonds and additional cranberries, if desired.

ROASTED PEPPER AND SOURDOUGH EGG DISH

Makes 6 servings

3 cups sourdough bread cubes

1 jar (12 ounces) roasted red pepper strips, drained

1 cup (4 ounces) shredded Monterey Jack cheese

1 cup (4 ounces) shredded sharp Cheddar cheese

1 cup cottage cheese

6 eggs

1 cup milk

¼ cup chopped fresh cilantro

¼ teaspoon black pepper

1. Coat inside of **CROCK-POT**® slow cooker with nonstick cooking spray. Add bread. Arrange roasted peppers evenly over bread cubes; sprinkle with Monterey Jack and Cheddar cheeses.

2. Place cottage cheese in food processor or blender; process until smooth. Add eggs and milk; process just until blended. Stir in cilantro and black pepper.

3. Pour egg mixture into **CROCK-POT**® slow cooker. Cover; cook on LOW 3 to 3½ hours or on HIGH 2 to 2½ hours or until eggs are firm but still moist.

BLUEBERRY-BANANA PANCAKES

Makes 8 servings

2 cups all-purpose flour

⅓ cup sugar

1 tablespoon baking powder

½ teaspoon baking soda

½ teaspoon salt

½ teaspoon ground cinnamon

1¾ cups milk

2 eggs, lightly beaten

¼ cup (½ stick) unsalted butter, melted

1 teaspoon vanilla

1 cup fresh blueberries

2 small bananas, sliced

Maple syrup (optional)

1. Combine flour, sugar, baking powder, baking soda, salt and cinnamon in large bowl. Combine milk, eggs, butter and vanilla in separate medium bowl. Pour milk mixture into flour mixture; stir until moistened. Gently fold in blueberries.

2. Coat inside of **CROCK-POT**® slow cooker with nonstick cooking spray. Pour batter into **CROCK-POT**® slow cooker. Cover; cook on HIGH 2 hours or until puffed and toothpick inserted into center comes out clean. Cut evenly into eight wedges; top with sliced bananas and syrup, if desired.

CHEESE GRITS WITH CHILES AND BACON

Makes 4 servings

6 slices bacon

1 serrano or jalapeño pepper, seeded and minced*

1 large shallot or small onion, finely chopped

4 cups chicken broth

1 cup grits**

Salt and black pepper

1 cup (4 ounces) shredded Cheddar cheese

½ cup half-and-half

2 tablespoons finely chopped green onion

*Serrano peppers can sting and irritate the skin, so wear rubber gloves when handling peppers and do not touch your eyes.

**Use coarse, instant, yellow or stone-ground grits.

1. Heat medium skillet over medium heat. Add bacon; cook and stir until crisp. Remove to paper towel-lined plate using slotted spoon. Cut two strips into 1-inch pieces; place in **CROCK-POT**® slow cooker. Refrigerate remaining bacon until ready to serve.

2. Drain all but 1 tablespoon bacon drippings from skillet. Add serrano pepper and shallot to skillet; cook and stir over medium-high heat 1 minute or until shallot is lightly browned. Remove to **CROCK-POT**® slow cooker. Stir broth, grits, black pepper and salt into **CROCK-POT**® slow cooker. Cover; cook on LOW 4 hours.

3. Stir in cheese and half-and-half. Chop remaining bacon into 1-inch pieces. Sprinkle bacon and green onion on top of each serving.

FRUIT OATMEAL

Makes 4 servings

4¼ cups water
1 cup steel-cut oats
¼ cup golden raisins
¼ cup dried cranberries
¼ cup dried cherries

2 tablespoons honey
1 teaspoon vanilla
¼ teaspoon salt
1 cup sliced fresh strawberries (optional)

Combine water, oats, raisins, cranberries, cherries, honey, vanilla and salt in **CROCK-POT**® slow cooker; stir to blend. Cover; cook on LOW 7 to 7½ hours. Top each serving evenly with strawberries, if desired.

BACON AND CHEESE BRUNCH POTATOES

Makes 6 servings

3 medium russet potatoes (about 2 pounds), peeled and cut into 1-inch cubes
1 cup chopped onion
½ teaspoon seasoned salt

4 slices bacon, crisp-cooked and crumbled
1 cup (4 ounces) shredded sharp Cheddar cheese
1 tablespoon water

1. Coat inside of **CROCK-POT**® slow cooker with nonstick cooking spray. Place half of potatoes in **CROCK-POT**® slow cooker. Sprinkle half of onion and seasoned salt over potatoes; top with half of bacon and cheese. Repeat layers. Sprinkle water over top.

2. Cover; cook on LOW 6 hours or on HIGH 3½ hours. Stir gently to mix.

CHOCOLATE-STUFFED FRENCH TOAST

Makes 6 servings

Butter, softened

6 slices (¾-inch-thick) day-old challah*

½ cup semisweet chocolate chips

6 eggs

3 cups half-and-half

⅔ cup granulated sugar

1 teaspoon vanilla

¼ teaspoon salt

Powdered sugar

Fresh fruit (optional)

*Challah is usually braided. If you use brioche or another rich egg bread, slice bread to fit baking dish.

1. Grease 2½-quart baking dish that fits inside of **CROCK-POT**® slow cooker with butter. Arrange 2 bread slices in bottom of dish. Sprinkle with ¼ cup chocolate chips. Add 2 more bread slices. Sprinkle with remaining ¼ cup chocolate chips. Top with remaining 2 bread slices.

2. Beat eggs in large bowl. Stir in half-and-half, granulated sugar, vanilla and salt. Pour egg mixture over bread layers. Press bread into liquid. Set aside 10 minutes or until liquid is absorbed. Cover dish with buttered foil, buttered side down.

3. Pour 1 inch hot water into **CROCK-POT**® slow cooker; add baking dish. Cover; cook on HIGH 3 hours or until toothpick inserted into center comes out clean. Remove dish and let stand 10 minutes. Sprinkle with powdered sugar. Garnish with fresh fruit.

TIP | Any oven-safe casserole or baking dish is safe to use in your **CROCK-POT**® slow cooker. Place directly inside the stoneware and follow the recipe directions.

APPLE-CINNAMON BREAKFAST RISOTTO

Makes 6 servings

¼ cup (½ stick) butter

4 medium Granny Smith apples (about 1½ pounds), peeled, cored and diced into ½-inch cubes

1½ teaspoons ground cinnamon

¼ teaspoon ground allspice

¼ teaspoon salt

1½ cups uncooked Arborio rice

½ cup packed dark brown sugar

4 cups unfiltered apple juice, at room temperature*

1 teaspoon vanilla

Optional toppings: dried cranberries, sliced almonds and/or milk

*If unfiltered apple juice is unavailable, use any apple juice.

1. Coat inside of **CROCK-POT**® slow cooker with nonstick cooking spray. Melt butter in large skillet over medium-high heat. Add apples, cinnamon, allspice and salt; cook and stir 3 to 5 minutes or until apples begin to release their juices. Remove to **CROCK-POT**® slow cooker.

2. Stir in rice. Sprinkle brown sugar evenly over top. Add apple juice and vanilla. Cover; cook on HIGH 1½ to 2 hours or until all liquid is absorbed. Ladle risotto into bowls; top as desired.

TIP | Keep the lid on! The **CROCK-POT**® slow cooker can take as long as 30 minutes to regain heat lost when the cover is removed.

MAPLE, BACON AND RASPBERRY PANCAKE

Makes 8 servings

5 slices bacon

2 cups pancake mix

1 cup water

½ cup maple syrup, plus additional for serving

1 cup fresh raspberries, plus additional for garnish

3 tablespoons chopped pecans, toasted*

To toast pecans, spread in single layer in heavy skillet. Cook and stir over medium heat 1 to 2 minutes or until nuts are lightly browned.

1. Heat large skillet over medium heat. Add bacon; cook and stir until crisp. Remove to paper towel-lined plate using slotted spoon; crumble.

2. Brush inside of 5-quart **CROCK-POT**® slow cooker with 1 to 2 tablespoons bacon fat from skillet. Combine pancake mix, water and ½ cup syrup in large bowl; stir to blend. Pour half of batter into **CROCK-POT**® slow cooker; top with ½ cup raspberries, half of bacon and half of pecans. Pour remaining half of batter over top; sprinkle with remaining ½ cup raspberries, bacon and pecans.

3. Cover; cook on HIGH 1½ to 2 hours or until pancake has risen and is cooked through. Turn off heat. Let stand, uncovered, 10 to 15 minutes. Remove pancake from **CROCK-POT**® slow cooker; cut into eight pieces. Serve with additional syrup and raspberries.

WAKE-UP POTATO AND SAUSAGE BREAKFAST CASSEROLE

Makes 8 servings

1 pound kielbasa or smoked sausage, diced

1 cup chopped onion

1 cup chopped red bell pepper

1 package (20 ounces) refrigerated Southwestern-style hash browns*

10 eggs

1 cup milk

1 cup (4 ounces) shredded Monterey Jack or sharp Cheddar cheese

You may substitute O'Brien potatoes and add ½ teaspoon chile powder.

1. Coat inside of **CROCK-POT**® slow cooker with nonstick cooking spray. Heat large skillet over medium-high heat. Add sausage and onion; cook and stir 6 to 8 minutes or until sausage is browned. Drain fat. Stir in bell pepper.

2. Place one third of potatoes in **CROCK-POT**® slow cooker. Top with half of sausage mixture. Repeat layers. Spread remaining one third of potatoes evenly on top.

3. Whisk eggs and milk in medium bowl. Pour evenly over potatoes. Cover; cook on LOW 6 to 7 hours.

4. Turn off heat. Sprinkle cheese over casserole; let stand 10 minutes or until cheese is melted.

TIP | To remove casserole from **CROCK-POT**® slow cooker, omit step 4. Run a rubber spatula around the edge of the casserole, lifting the bottom slightly. Invert onto a large plate. Place a large serving platter on top; invert again. Sprinkle with cheese and let stand until cheese is melted. To serve, cut into wedges.

BLUEBERRY-ORANGE FRENCH TOAST CASSEROLE

Makes 6 servings

½ cup sugar

½ cup milk

2 eggs

4 egg whites

1 tablespoon grated orange peel

½ teaspoon vanilla

6 slices whole wheat bread, cut into 1-inch cubes

1 cup fresh blueberries

Maple syrup (optional)

1. Coat inside of **CROCK-POT**® slow cooker with nonstick cooking spray. Stir sugar and milk in large bowl until sugar is dissolved. Whisk in eggs, egg whites, orange peel and vanilla. Add bread and blueberries; stir to coat.

2. Remove mixture to **CROCK-POT**® slow cooker. Cover; cook on LOW 3 to 4 hours or on HIGH 1½ to 2 hours or until toothpick inserted into center comes out mostly clean.

3. Turn off heat. Let stand 10 minutes. Serve with syrup, if desired.

APPLE AND GRANOLA BREAKFAST COBBLER

Makes 4 servings

4 Granny Smith apples, peeled, cored and sliced

½ cup packed light brown sugar

1 tablespoon lemon juice

1 teaspoon ground cinnamon

2 cups granola cereal, plus additional for garnish

2 tablespoons butter, cut into small pieces

Whipping cream, half-and-half or vanilla yogurt (optional)

1. Place apples in **CROCK-POT**® slow cooker. Sprinkle brown sugar, lemon juice and cinnamon over apples. Stir in 2 cups granola and butter.

2. Cover; cook on LOW 6 hours or on HIGH 2 to 3 hours. Serve warm with additional granola sprinkled on top. Serve with cream, if desired.

BREAKFAST QUINOA

Makes 6 servings

1½ cups uncooked quinoa

3 cups water

3 tablespoons packed brown sugar

2 tablespoons maple syrup

1½ teaspoons ground cinnamon

¾ cup golden raisins

Fresh raspberries and banana slices

1. Place quinoa in fine-mesh strainer; rinse well under cold running water. Remove to **CROCK-POT**® slow cooker.

2. Stir water, brown sugar, syrup and cinnamon into **CROCK-POT**® slow cooker. Cover; cook on LOW 5 hours or on HIGH 2½ hours or until quinoa is tender and water is absorbed.

3. Add raisins during last 10 to 15 minutes of cooking time. Top quinoa with raspberries and bananas.

BRAN MUFFIN BREAD

Makes 1 loaf

2 cups all-bran cereal

2 cups whole wheat flour*

2 teaspoons baking powder

1 teaspoon baking soda

¼ teaspoon ground cinnamon

½ teaspoon salt

1 egg

1½ cups buttermilk

¼ cup molasses

¼ cup (½ stick) unsalted butter, melted

1 cup chopped walnuts

½ cup raisins

Honey (optional)

*For proper texture of finished bread, spoon flour into measuring cup and level off. Do not dip into bag, pack down flour or tap on counter to level when measuring.

1. Butter and flour 8-cup mold that fits inside of 6-quart **CROCK-POT**® slow cooker. Combine cereal, flour, baking powder, baking soda, cinnamon and salt in large bowl.

2. Beat egg in medium bowl. Whisk in buttermilk, molasses and melted butter. Stir into flour mixture just until combined. Stir in walnuts and raisins. Spoon batter into prepared mold. Cover with buttered foil, buttered side down.

3. Place rack in **CROCK-POT**® slow cooker. Pour 1 inch hot water into **CROCK-POT**® slow cooker (water should not come to top of rack). Place mold on rack. Cover; cook on LOW 3½ to 4 hours or until bread starts to pull away from side of mold and toothpick inserted into center comes out clean. (If necessary, replace foil. Cover; cook on LOW 45 minutes.)

4. Remove mold from **CROCK-POT**® slow cooker. Let stand 10 minutes. Remove foil and run rubber spatula around outer edge, lifting bottom slightly to loosen. Invert bread onto wire rack. Serve warm with honey, if desired.

TIP | Cooking times are guidelines. **CROCK-POT**® slow cookers, just like ovens, cook differently depending on the recipe size and the individual **CROCK-POT**® slow cooker. Always check for doneness before serving.

BREAKFAST BERRY BREAD PUDDING

Makes 10 to 12 servings

6 cups bread, preferably sourdough, cut into ¾- to 1-inch cubes

1 cup raisins

½ cup slivered almonds, toasted*

6 eggs, beaten

1½ cups packed light brown sugar

1¾ cups milk

1½ teaspoons ground cinnamon

1 teaspoon vanilla

3 cups sliced fresh strawberries

2 cups fresh blueberries

Fresh mint leaves (optional)

*To toast almonds, spread in single layer in heavy skillet. Cook over medium heat 1 to 2 minutes or until nuts are lightly browned, stirring frequently.

1. Coat inside of **CROCK-POT**® slow cooker with nonstick cooking spray. Add bread, raisins and almonds; toss to combine.

2. Whisk eggs, brown sugar, milk, cinnamon and vanilla in separate bowl. Pour egg mixture over bread mixture; toss to blend. Cover; cook on LOW 4 to 4½ hours or on HIGH 3 hours.

3. Remove stoneware from **CROCK-POT**® base. Allow bread pudding to cool and set before serving. Serve with berries; garnish with mint.

MEDITERRANEAN FRITTATA

Makes 4 to 6 servings

Butter, softened

3 tablespoons extra virgin olive oil

1 large onion, chopped

8 ounces (about 2 cups) sliced mushrooms

6 cloves garlic, sliced

1 teaspoon dried basil

1 medium red bell pepper, chopped

1 package (10 ounces) frozen chopped spinach, thawed and squeezed dry

¼ cup sliced kalamata olives

8 eggs, beaten

4 ounces feta cheese, crumbled

½ teaspoon salt

¼ teaspoon black pepper

1. Coat inside lower third of 5- to 6-quart **CROCK-POT**® slow cooker with butter. Heat oil in large skillet over medium-high heat. Add onion, mushrooms, garlic and basil; cook 2 to 3 minutes or until slightly softened, stirring occasionally. Add bell pepper; cook 4 to 5 minutes or until vegetables are tender. Stir in spinach; cook 2 minutes. Stir in olives. Remove onion mixture to **CROCK-POT**® slow cooker.

2. Whisk eggs, cheese, salt and black pepper in large bowl. Pour over vegetables in **CROCK-POT**® slow cooker. Cover; cook on LOW 2½ to 3 hours or on HIGH 1¼ to 1½ hours or until eggs are set. Cut into wedges to serve.

APPLE-CRANBERRY CRÊPES

Makes 4 servings

1 baking apple, such as Gala or Jonathan, peeled, cored and cut into 6 wedges

1 tart apple, such as Granny Smith, peeled, cored and cut into 6 wedges

¼ cup dried sweetened cranberries or cherries

2 tablespoons lemon juice

½ teaspoon plus ⅛ teaspoon ground cinnamon, divided

⅛ teaspoon ground nutmeg

⅛ teaspoon ground cloves or allspice

1 tablespoon butter

¼ cup orange juice

1 tablespoon sugar

¾ teaspoon cornstarch

¼ teaspoon almond extract

4 prepared crêpes

Vanilla ice cream (optional)

1. Coat inside of **CROCK-POT**® slow cooker with nonstick cooking spray. Place apples, cranberries, lemon juice, ½ teaspoon cinnamon, nutmeg and cloves in **CROCK-POT**® slow cooker; toss to coat. Cover; cook on LOW 2 hours. Stir butter into apple mixture just until melted.

2. Stir orange juice, sugar, cornstarch and almond extract in small bowl until cornstarch dissolves. Stir into apple mixture in **CROCK-POT**® slow cooker. Turn **CROCK-POT**® slow cooker to HIGH. Cover; cook on HIGH 15 minutes or until sauce thickens slightly.

3. Place 1 crêpe on each of four dessert plates. Spoon apple mixture evenly down center of each crêpe. Fold edges over; turn crêpes with seam side down on plates. Sprinkle with remaining ⅛ teaspoon cinnamon. Microwave filled crêpes according to package directions, if desired. Serve with ice cream, if desired.

TIP | Look for prepared crêpes in the produce section of the supermarket.

APPETIZERS AND SNACKS

PARMESAN RANCH SNACK MIX

Makes about 9½ cups

3 cups corn or rice cereal squares

2 cups oyster crackers

1 package (5 ounces) bagel chips, broken in half

1½ cups mini pretzel twists

1 cup pistachio nuts

2 tablespoons grated Parmesan cheese

¼ cup (½ stick) butter, melted

1 package (1 ounce) dry ranch salad dressing mix

½ teaspoon garlic powder

1. Combine cereal, crackers, bagel chips, pretzels, pistachios and cheese in **CROCK-POT®** slow cooker; mix gently.

2. Combine butter, salad dressing mix and garlic powder in small bowl; stir to blend. Pour over cereal mixture; toss lightly to coat. Cover; cook on LOW 3 hours.

3. Stir gently. Cook, uncovered, on LOW 30 minutes.

SPICY SWEET AND SOUR COCKTAIL FRANKS

Makes 10 to 12 servings

2 packages (8 ounces *each*)
  beef cocktail franks

½ cup ketchup or chili sauce

½ cup apricot preserves

1 teaspoon hot pepper sauce

Coat inside of **CROCK-POT**® slow cooker with nonstick cooking spray. Combine cocktail franks, ketchup, preserves and hot pepper sauce in **CROCK-POT**® slow cooker; stir to blend. Cover; cook on LOW 2 to 3 hours.

STEWED FIG AND BLUE CHEESE DIP

Makes 6 to 8 servings

1 tablespoon olive oil

1 medium onion, chopped

½ cup port wine

1 package (6 ounces) dried Calimyrna figs, finely chopped, plus additional fig halves for garnish

½ cup orange juice

½ cup crumbled blue cheese, divided

1 tablespoon unsalted butter

Assorted crackers and grapes

1. Heat oil in small skillet over medium-high heat. Add onion; cook and stir 7 to 8 minutes or until light golden. Stir in port. Bring to a boil; cook 1 minute. Remove to **CROCK-POT**® slow cooker; stir in 1 package figs and orange juice.

2. Cover; cook on LOW 1 to 1½ hours or until figs are plump and tender. Stir in ¼ cup blue cheese and butter. Sprinkle with remaining blue cheese. Garnish with additional fig halves. Serve with crackers and grapes.

BEANS AND SPINACH BRUSCHETTA

Makes 16 servings

2 cans (about 15 ounces *each*)
   Great Northern or cannellini
   beans, rinsed and drained

3 cloves garlic, minced
   Salt and black pepper

6 cups spinach, loosely packed
   and finely chopped

1 tablespoon red wine vinegar

2 tablespoons extra virgin olive
   oil

16 slices whole grain baguette

1. Combine beans, garlic, salt and black pepper in **CROCK-POT®** slow cooker; stir to blend. Cover; cook on LOW 3 hours or until beans are tender. Turn off heat. Mash beans with potato masher. Stir in spinach and vinegar.

2. Preheat broiler. Brush baguette slices with oil. Broil 5 to 7 minutes or until bread is golden brown and crisp. Top with bean mixture and spinach.

HOISIN SRIRACHA CHICKEN WINGS

Makes 5 to 6 servings

3 pounds chicken wings, tips removed and split at joints

½ cup hoisin sauce

¼ cup plus 1 tablespoon sriracha sauce, divided

2 tablespoons packed brown sugar

Chopped green onions (optional)

1. Coat inside of **CROCK-POT**® slow cooker with nonstick cooking spray. Preheat broiler. Spray large baking sheet with cooking spray. Arrange wings on prepared baking sheet. Broil 6 to 8 minutes or until browned, turning once. Remove wings to **CROCK-POT**® slow cooker.

2. Combine hoisin sauce, ¼ cup sriracha sauce and brown sugar in medium bowl; stir to blend. Pour sauce mixture over wings in **CROCK-POT**® slow cooker; stir to coat. Cover; cook on LOW 3½ to 4 hours. Remove wings to large serving platter; cover with foil to keep warm.

3. Turn **CROCK-POT**® slow cooker to HIGH. Cook, uncovered, on HIGH 10 to 15 minutes or until sauce is thickened. Stir in remaining 1 tablespoon sriracha sauce. Spoon sauce over wings to serve. Garnish with green onions.

BARBECUE BEEF SLIDERS

Makes 6 servings

1 tablespoon packed light
  brown sugar

1 teaspoon ground cumin

1 teaspoon chili powder

1 teaspoon paprika

½ teaspoon salt

¼ teaspoon ground red pepper

3 pounds beef short ribs

½ cup plus 2 tablespoons
  barbecue sauce, divided

¼ cup water

12 slider rolls

¾ cup prepared coleslaw

12 bread and butter pickle chips

1. Coat inside of **CROCK-POT®** slow cooker with nonstick cooking spray. Combine brown sugar, cumin, chili powder, paprika, salt and ground red pepper in small bowl. Rub over ribs; remove to **CROCK-POT®** slow cooker. Pour in ½ cup barbecue sauce and water.

2. Cover; cook on LOW 7 to 8 hours or on HIGH 4 to 4½ hours or until ribs are very tender and meat shreds easily. Remove ribs to large cutting board. Discard bones; remove meat to large bowl. Shred meat using two forks, discarding any large pieces of fat or sinew. Stir in remaining 2 tablespoons barbecue sauce and 2 tablespoons liquid from **CROCK-POT®** slow cooker.

3. Arrange bottom half of rolls on platter or work surface. Top each with ¼ cup beef mixture, 1 tablespoon coleslaw and 1 pickle chip. Place roll tops on each.

TIP | To remove any sticky barbecue sauce residue, soak the **CROCK-POT®** stoneware in hot sudsy water. Then scrub it with a plastic or nylon scrubber. Don't use steel wool.

BACON-WRAPPED DATES

Makes 8 to 10 servings

4 ounces goat cheese or blue cheese

1 package (8 ounces) dried pitted dates

1 pound thick-cut bacon (about 11 slices), halved

1. Fill **CROCK-POT**® slow cooker with about ½-inch water. Spoon goat cheese evenly into centers of dates; close. Wrap half slice of bacon around each date; secure with toothpicks.

2. Heat large skillet over medium heat. Add wrapped dates; cook and turn 5 to 10 minutes until browned. Remove to **CROCK-POT**® slow cooker.

3. Cover; cook on LOW 2 to 3 hours. Remove toothpicks before serving.

BARLEY "CAVIAR"

Makes 8 appetizers

4½ cups water

¾ cup uncooked pearl barley

1 teaspoon salt, divided

½ cup sliced pimiento-stuffed olives

½ cup finely chopped red bell pepper

1 stalk celery, chopped

1 large shallot, finely chopped

1 jalapeño pepper,* minced, *or* ¼ teaspoon red pepper flakes

2 tablespoons plus 1 teaspoon olive oil

4 teaspoons white wine vinegar

¼ teaspoon ground cumin

⅛ teaspoon black pepper

8 leaves endive or Bibb lettuce

Jalapeño peppers can sting and irritate the skin, so wear rubber gloves when handling peppers and do not touch your eyes.

1. Add water, barley and ½ teaspoon salt to **CROCK-POT**® slow cooker. Cover; cook on LOW 4 to 5 hours or on HIGH 2½ to 3 hours or until barley is tender and liquid is absorbed.

2. Turn off heat. Stir in olives, bell pepper, celery, shallot and jalapeño pepper. Combine oil, vinegar, remaining ½ teaspoon salt, cumin and black pepper in small bowl; stir well. Pour over barley mixture in **CROCK-POT**® slow cooker; stir gently to coat. Let stand 10 minutes. To serve, spoon barley mixture evenly into endive leaves.

MINI MEATBALL GRINDERS

Makes 12 servings

1 can (about 14 ounces) diced tomatoes, drained and juices reserved

1 can (8 ounces) tomato sauce

¼ cup chopped onion

2 tablespoons tomato paste

1 teaspoon Italian seasoning

1 pound ground chicken

½ cup fresh whole wheat or white bread crumbs (1 slice bread)

1 egg white, lightly beaten

3 tablespoons finely chopped fresh Italian parsley

2 cloves garlic, minced

¼ teaspoon salt

⅛ teaspoon black pepper
Nonstick cooking spray

4 hard rolls, split and toasted

3 tablespoons grated Parmesan cheese (optional)

1. Combine tomatoes, ½ cup reserved juice, tomato sauce, onion, tomato paste and Italian seasoning in **CROCK-POT**® slow cooker. Cover; cook on LOW 3 to 4 hours.

2. Prepare meatballs halfway through cooking time. Combine chicken, bread crumbs, egg white, parsley, garlic, salt and pepper in medium bowl; mix well. Shape mixture into 12 meatballs. Cover; refrigerate 30 minutes.

3. Spray medium skillet with cooking spray; heat over medium heat. Add meatballs; cook 8 to 10 minutes or until well browned on all sides. Remove meatballs to **CROCK-POT**® slow cooker using slotted spoon. Cover; cook on LOW 1 to 2 hours or until no longer pink in center.

4. Place 3 meatballs in each roll; top with sauce. Sprinkle with cheese, if desired. Cut each roll into thirds.

ANGELIC DEVILED EGGS

Makes 12 servings

6 eggs

¼ cup cottage cheese

3 tablespoons ranch dressing

2 teaspoons Dijon mustard

2 tablespoons minced fresh chives or dill

1 tablespoon diced well-drained pimientos or roasted red pepper

1. Place eggs in single layer in bottom of **CROCK-POT**® slow cooker; add just enough water to cover tops of eggs. Cover; cook on LOW 3½ hours. Rinse and drain eggs under cold running water; peel when cool enough to handle.

2. Cut eggs in half lengthwise. Remove yolks, reserving 3 yolk halves. Discard remaining yolks or reserve for another use. Place egg whites, cut sides up, on serving plate; cover with plastic wrap. Refrigerate while preparing filling.

3. Combine cottage cheese, dressing, mustard and reserved yolk halves in food processor or blender; process until smooth. (Or, place in small bowl and mash with fork until well blended.) Remove cheese mixture to small bowl; stir in chives and pimientos. Spoon into egg whites. Cover; refrigerate at least 1 hour before serving.

THAI CHICKEN WINGS

Makes 8 to 10 servings

1 tablespoon peanut oil

5 pounds chicken wings, tips removed and split at joints

½ cup unsweetened canned coconut milk

1 tablespoon sugar

1 tablespoon Thai green curry paste

1 tablespoon fish sauce

¾ cup prepared spicy peanut sauce

Sliced green onions (optional)

1. Heat oil in large skillet over medium-high heat. Add wings in batches; cook 3 to 5 minutes or until browned on all sides. Remove to **CROCK-POT**® slow cooker using slotted spoon.

2. Stir coconut milk, sugar, curry paste and fish sauce into **CROCK-POT**® slow cooker. Cover; cook on LOW 6 to 7 hours or on HIGH 3 to 3½ hours. Remove wings with slotted spoon to large bowl; toss with peanut sauce before serving. Garnish with green onions.

SHRIMP FONDUE DIP

Makes 5 cups

1 pound medium raw shrimp, peeled and deveined

½ cup water

½ teaspoon salt, divided

2 tablespoons butter, softened

4 teaspoons Dijon mustard

6 slices thick-sliced white bread, crusts removed

1 cup milk

2 eggs, beaten

¼ teaspoon black pepper

2 cups (8 ounces) shredded Gruyère or Swiss cheese

French bread slices

1. Coat inside of **CROCK-POT**® slow cooker with nonstick cooking spray. Place shrimp, water and ¼ teaspoon salt in large saucepan. Cover; cook over medium heat 3 minutes or until shrimp are pink and opaque. Drain shrimp, reserving ½ cup broth.

2. Combine butter and mustard in small bowl; stir to blend. Spread mixture onto bread slices. Cut bread into 1-inch cubes.

3. Beat milk, eggs, reserved ½ cup broth, remaining ¼ teaspoon salt and pepper in medium bowl until well blended.

4. Spread one third of bread cubes in bottom of **CROCK-POT**® slow cooker. Top with one third of shrimp and sprinkle with one third of cheese. Repeat layers twice. Pour egg mixture over top. Press down on bread mixture to absorb liquid. Line lid with two paper towels. Cover; cook on LOW 2 hours or until mixture is heated through and thickened. Serve with French bread.

TIP | For a party, use a **CROCK-POT**® slow cooker on the LOW or WARM setting to keep hot dips and fondues warm.

PARTY MEATBALLS

Makes 10 to 12 servings

1 package (about 1 pound) frozen cocktail-size turkey or beef meatballs

½ cup maple syrup

1 jar (12 ounces) chili sauce

1 jar (12 ounces) grape jelly

Place meatballs, syrup, chili sauce and jelly in **CROCK-POT**® slow cooker; stir to blend. Cover; cook on LOW 3 to 4 hours or on HIGH 2 to 3 hours.

CHIPOTLE TURKEY SLOPPY JOE SLIDERS

Makes 12 sliders

1 pound turkey Italian sausage, casings removed

1 package (14 ounces) frozen green and red bell pepper strips with onions

1 can (6 ounces) tomato paste

1 tablespoon quick-cooking tapioca

1 tablespoon minced canned chipotle peppers in adobo sauce, plus 1 tablespoon sauce

2 teaspoons ground cumin

½ teaspoon dried thyme

12 corn muffins or small dinner rolls, split and toasted

1. Brown sausage in large skillet over medium-high heat 6 to 8 minutes, stirring to break up meat. Remove to **CROCK-POT**® slow cooker using slotted spoon.

2. Stir in pepper strips with onions, tomato paste, tapioca, chipotle peppers with sauce, cumin and thyme. Cover; cook on LOW 8 to 10 hours. Serve on corn muffins.

CHICKEN AND ASIAGO STUFFED MUSHROOMS

Makes 4 to 5 servings

20 large white mushrooms, stems removed and reserved

3 tablespoons extra virgin olive oil, divided

¼ cup finely chopped onion

2 cloves garlic, minced

¼ cup Madeira wine

½ pound chicken sausage, casings removed or ground chicken

1 cup grated Asiago cheese

¼ cup Italian-style seasoned dry bread crumbs

3 tablespoons chopped fresh Italian parsley

½ teaspoon salt

¼ teaspoon black pepper

1. Lightly brush mushroom caps with 1 tablespoon oil; set aside. Finely chop mushroom stems.

2. Heat remaining 2 tablespoons oil in large nonstick skillet over medium-high heat. Add onion; cook 1 minute or until just beginning to soften. Add mushroom stems; cook 5 to 6 minutes or until beginning to brown. Stir in garlic; cook 1 minute.

3. Pour in wine; cook 1 minute. Add sausage; cook 3 to 4 minutes or until no longer pink, stirring to break up meat. Remove from heat; cool 5 minutes. Stir in cheese, bread crumbs, parsley, salt and pepper.

4. Divide mushroom-sausage mixture among mushroom caps, pressing slightly to compress. Place stuffed mushroom caps in single layer in **CROCK-POT**® slow cooker. Cover; cook on LOW 4 hours or on HIGH 2 hours.

TIP | Stuffed mushrooms are a great way to impress guests with your gourmet cooking skills. These appetizers appear time intensive and fancy, but they are actually simple with the help of a **CROCK-POT**® slow cooker.

MINI CARNITAS TACOS

Makes 12 servings

1½ pounds boneless pork loin, cut into 1-inch cubes

1 onion, finely chopped

½ cup chicken broth

1 tablespoon chili powder

2 teaspoons ground cumin

1 teaspoon dried oregano

½ teaspoon minced canned chipotle peppers in adobo sauce

½ cup pico de gallo

2 tablespoons chopped fresh cilantro

½ teaspoon salt

12 (6-inch) corn or flour tortillas

¾ cup (3 ounces) shredded sharp Cheddar cheese

3 tablespoons sour cream

1. Combine pork, onion, broth, chili powder, cumin, oregano and chipotle peppers in **CROCK-POT®** slow cooker; stir to blend. Cover; cook on LOW 6 hours or on HIGH 3 hours. Pour off excess cooking liquid.

2. Remove pork to large cutting board; shred with two forks. Return to **CROCK-POT®** slow cooker. Stir in pico de gallo, cilantro and salt. Cover; keep warm on LOW or WARM setting.

3. Cut three circles from each tortilla with 2-inch biscuit cutter. Top each with pork, cheese and sour cream. Serve warm.

TIP | Carnitas, or "little meats" in Spanish, are a festive way to spice up any gathering. Carnitas traditionally include a large amount of lard, but slow cooking makes the dish healthier by eliminating the need to add lard, oil or fat, while keeping the meat tender and delicious.

CHIPOTLE CHILI CON QUESO DIP

Makes 1½ cups

10 ounces pasteurized process cheese product, cubed

¼ cup mild chunky salsa

½ canned chipotle pepper in adobo sauce, finely chopped*

½ teaspoon Worcestershire sauce

⅛ teaspoon chili powder

Pretzels

Use more to taste.

1. Coat inside of **CROCK-POT**® slow cooker with nonstick cooking spray. Combine cheese product, salsa, chipotle pepper, Worcestershire sauce and chili powder in **CROCK-POT**® slow cooker. Cover; cook on LOW 1 hour.

2. Stir well. Cover; cook on LOW 30 minutes or until cheese is melted. Stir until smooth. Serve with pretzels.

SOUPS AND STOCKS

CHICKEN ORZO SOUP

Makes 6 to 8 servings

1 tablespoon vegetable oil

1 onion, diced

1 fennel bulb, quartered, cored, thinly sliced, tops removed and fronds reserved for garnish

2 teaspoons minced garlic

8 cups chicken broth

2 boneless, skinless chicken breasts (8 ounces *each*)

2 carrots, peeled and thinly sliced

2 sprigs fresh thyme

1 whole bay leaf

Salt and black pepper

½ cup uncooked orzo

1. Heat oil in large skillet over medium heat. Add onion and fennel; cook 8 minutes or until tender. Add garlic; cook and stir 1 minute. Remove to **CROCK-POT**® slow cooker. Add broth, chicken, carrots, thyme and bay leaf. Season with salt and pepper; stir to blend. Cover; cook on HIGH 2 to 3 hours.

2. Remove chicken to large cutting board; shred with two forks. Add orzo to **CROCK-POT**® slow cooker. Cover; cook on HIGH 30 minutes. Stir shredded chicken back into **CROCK-POT**® slow cooker. Remove and discard thyme sprigs and bay leaf. Garnish each serving with fennel fronds.

BEEF AND BEET BORSCHT

Makes 6 to 8 servings

6 slices bacon

1 boneless beef chuck roast (1½ pounds), trimmed and cut into ½-inch pieces

1 medium onion, chopped

4 cloves garlic, minced

4 medium beets, peeled and cut into ½-inch pieces

3 cups beef broth

2 large carrots, sliced

6 sprigs fresh dill

3 tablespoons honey

3 tablespoons red wine vinegar

2 whole bay leaves

3 cups shredded green cabbage

1. Heat large skillet over medium heat. Add bacon; cook and stir until crisp. Remove to paper towel-lined plate using slotted spoon; crumble.

2. Return skillet to medium-high heat. Add beef; cook 5 minutes or until browned. Remove beef to **CROCK-POT**® slow cooker.

3. Pour off all but 1 tablespoon fat from skillet. Add onion and garlic; cook 4 minutes or until onion is softened. Remove onion mixture to **CROCK-POT**® slow cooker. Stir in beets, broth, carrots, bacon, dill, honey, vinegar and bay leaves.

4. Cover; cook on LOW 5 to 6 hours. Stir in cabbage. Cover; cook on LOW 30 minutes. Remove and discard bay leaves before serving.

ASIAN SUGAR SNAP PEA SOUP

Makes 4 servings

2 tablespoons peanut or canola oil

4 to 5 new potatoes, coarsely chopped

2 green onions, chopped

1 medium carrot, thinly sliced

1 stalk celery, thinly sliced

1 leek, thinly sliced

5 cups water

2 cups broccoli, cut into florets

1 tablespoon lemon juice

1 tablespoon soy sauce

1 teaspoon ground coriander

1 teaspoon ground cumin

1 teaspoon prepared horseradish

⅛ teaspoon ground red pepper

1 cup fresh sugar snap peas, shelled, rinsed and drained

4 cups cooked brown rice

1. Heat oil in large skillet over medium heat. Add potatoes, green onions, carrot, celery and leek; cook and stir 10 to 12 minutes or until vegetables begin to soften.

2. Remove to **CROCK-POT**® slow cooker. Add water, broccoli, lemon juice, soy sauce, coriander, cumin, horseradish and ground red pepper. Cover; cook on LOW 5 to 6 hours or on HIGH 2 to 3 hours.

3. Stir in peas. Cover; cook on HIGH 15 minutes or until peas are crisp-tender. To serve, portion rice into four bowls. Ladle soup over rice and serve immediately.

CREAMY CRAB BISQUE

Makes 6 to 8 servings

4 cups whipping cream

3 cups fresh crabmeat, flaked and picked over for shells

3 tablespoons unsalted butter

2 teaspoons grated lemon peel

1 teaspoon lemon juice

½ teaspoon ground nutmeg

¼ teaspoon ground allspice

3 tablespoons dry red wine

½ cup prepared mandlen (soup nuts), ground into crumbs*

Mandlen are small nugget-like crackers made from matzo meal, available in the supermarket ethnic foods aisle.

1. Combine cream, crabmeat, butter, lemon peel, lemon juice, nutmeg and allspice in **CROCK-POT®** slow cooker; stir to blend. Cover; cook on LOW 1 to 2 hours.

2. Stir in wine and mandlen crumbs. Cover; cook on LOW 10 minutes.

BROCCOLI CHEDDAR SOUP

Makes 6 servings

3 tablespoons butter

1 medium onion, chopped

3 tablespoons all-purpose flour

¼ teaspoon ground nutmeg

¼ teaspoon black pepper

4 cups vegetable broth

1 large bunch broccoli, chopped

1 medium red potato, peeled and chopped

1 teaspoon salt

1 whole bay leaf

1½ cups (6 ounces) shredded Cheddar cheese, plus additional for garnish

½ cup whipping cream

1. Melt butter in medium saucepan over medium heat. Add onion; cook and stir 6 minutes or until softened. Add flour, nutmeg and pepper; cook and stir 1 minute. Remove to **CROCK-POT**® slow cooker. Stir in broth, broccoli, potato, salt and bay leaf.

2. Cover; cook on HIGH 3 hours. Remove and discard bay leaf. Add soup in batches to food processor or blender; purée until desired consistency. Pour soup back into **CROCK-POT**® slow cooker. Stir in 1½ cups cheese and cream until cheese is melted. Garnish with additional cheese.

BEEF STOCK

Makes 8 to 10 cups

3 to 4 tablespoons vegetable oil, divided

3 to 4 pounds beef bones, preferably marrow or knuckle bones

9 cups water, divided

2 large leeks, thoroughly cleaned and cut into 1-inch pieces

3 carrots, cut into 1-inch pieces

3 cups onions, coarsely chopped

2 stalks celery, cut into 1-inch pieces

1 tablespoon tomato paste

2 sprigs fresh thyme

2 large sprigs fresh Italian parsley

1 whole bay leaf

½ tablespoon black peppercorns

1. Preheat oven to 450°F. Coat large roasting pan with 1 to 2 tablespoons oil. Arrange bones in single layer in pan. Roast in middle of oven 30 to 45 minutes or until browned, turning once or twice.

2. Remove bones to **CROCK-POT**® slow cooker using tongs. Add 8 cups water. Discard fat from roasting pan. Add ½ cup water to roasting pan, stirring and scraping up any brown bits. Add to **CROCK-POT**® slow cooker. Cover; cook on LOW 8 to 10 hours or on HIGH 5 to 6 hours.

3. In last hour of cooking, preheat oven to 450°F. Coat roasting pan with remaining 1 to 2 tablespoons oil and arrange leeks, carrots, onions and celery in single layer. Roast in middle of oven, 20 to 30 minutes or until golden brown, stirring once. Remove vegetables to **CROCK-POT**® slow cooker. Add remaining ½ cup water to hot pan, stirring and scraping up any brown bits. Add to **CROCK-POT**® slow cooker. Add tomato paste, thyme, parsley, bay leaf and peppercorns; stir to blend. Cover; cook on HIGH 2 hours.

4. Strain stock and discard solids. Allow stock to cool to room temperature; place in refrigerator overnight. Discard any fat that rises to top of chilled stock before using or freezing.

BACON-MUSHROOM SOUP

Makes 6 to 8 servings

Nonstick cooking spray

2½ packages (8 ounces *each*) mushrooms, chopped

3 carrots, chopped (about 1½ cups)

2 stalks celery, chopped (about 1 cup)

1 medium onion, chopped (about 1 cup)

2 large shallots, chopped (about ½ cup)

1 teaspoon dried oregano

4 cups beef broth

7 slices bacon, crisp-cooked and chopped, divided

2 tablespoons tomato paste

2 tablespoons soy sauce

¼ teaspoon black pepper

1. Spray large skillet with cooking spray; heat over medium-high heat. Add mushrooms; cook and stir 3 to 4 minutes or until softened. Add carrots, celery, onion, shallots and oregano; cook and stir 2 minutes. Remove mushroom mixture to **CROCK-POT**® slow cooker using slotted spoon. Stir in broth, 5 tablespoons bacon, tomato paste and soy sauce.

2. Cover; cook on LOW 6 to 7 hours or on HIGH 3 to 3½ hours or until vegetables are tender. Remove 4 cups soup to food processor or blender; process until smooth. Return to **CROCK-POT**® slow cooker; stir in pepper. Top with remaining 2 tablespoons bacon.

CHICKEN TORTILLA SOUP

Makes 4 to 6 servings

2 cans (about 14 ounces *each*) diced tomatoes

1 can (4 ounces) diced mild green chiles, drained

1 cup chicken broth, divided

1 yellow onion, diced

2 cloves garlic, minced

1 teaspoon ground cumin

4 boneless, skinless chicken thighs

Salt and black pepper

4 corn tortillas, sliced into ¼-inch strips

2 tablespoons chopped fresh cilantro

½ cup (2 ounces) shredded Monterey Jack cheese

1 avocado, diced and tossed with lime juice

Lime wedges

1. Combine tomatoes, chiles, ½ cup broth, onion, garlic and cumin in **CROCK-POT**® slow cooker; stir to blend. Add chicken. Cover; cook on LOW 6 hours or on HIGH 3 hours.

2. Remove chicken to large cutting board; shred with two forks. Return to cooking liquid. Season with salt, pepper and additional ½ cup broth, if necessary.

3. Just before serving, add tortillas and cilantro to **CROCK-POT**® slow cooker; stir to blend. Top each serving with cheese, avocado and a squeeze of lime juice.

CHICKEN STOCK

Makes about 10 cups

1 cut up whole chicken (4 to 6 pounds)

1 package (16 ounces) celery, cut into large pieces

1 large carrot, cut into 2- to 3-inch pieces

2 onions or leeks, quartered

2 large parsnips, coarsely chopped

½ cup loosely packed fresh herbs such as Italian parsley, dill, thyme, chervil or combination

Kosher salt and black pepper

1. Combine chicken, celery, carrot, onions, parsnips, herbs, salt and pepper in **CROCK-POT**® slow cooker. Add enough water to fill three-quarters full. Cover; cook on LOW 12 hours or on HIGH 8 hours.

2. Strain stock and discard solids. Allow stock to cool to room temperature; place in refrigerator overnight. Discard any fat that rises to top of chilled stock before using or freezing.

POSOLE

Makes 8 servings

3 pounds boneless pork loin, cubed

2 cans (about 15 ounces *each*) white hominy, rinsed and drained

1 package (10 ounces) frozen white corn, thawed

1 cup chili sauce

Combine pork, hominy, corn and chili sauce in **CROCK-POT**® slow cooker; stir to blend. Cover; cook on LOW 10 hours or on HIGH 5 hours.

VEGETABLE STOCK

Makes 10 to 12 cups

3 carrots, coarsely chopped

3 parsnips, coarsely chopped

3 onions, quartered

3 leeks, coarsely chopped

3 stalks celery, coarsely chopped

3 whole bay leaves

2 sprigs fresh thyme

4 sprigs fresh Italian parsley

8 whole black peppercorns

Water

Kosher salt

1. Add carrots, parsnips, onions, leeks, celery, bay leaves, thyme, parsley and peppercorns to **CROCK-POT**® slow cooker and fill three-quarters full with water. Season with salt. Cover; cook on LOW 10 to 12 hours or on HIGH 6 to 8 hours.

2. Strain stock and discard solids. Allow stock to cool to room temperature and refrigerate, freeze or use immediately.

NOTE: This recipe calls for bay leaves, thyme and parsley, but any combination of herbs and spices can be used to create a signature broth for a special soup. Try a variety of classic herbs and spices such as rosemary, sage, parsley and chives, or experiment with more exotic varieties such as Thai basil, mint, cilantro, ginger, lemongrass and star anise. Varying the vegetables to suit the soup also offers limitless possibilities with additions such as turnip, sweet potato, yam, rutabaga, celery root, fennel and mushrooms.

ROASTED TOMATO-BASIL SOUP

Makes 6 servings

2 cans (28 ounces *each*) whole tomatoes, drained, 3 cups liquid reserved

2½ tablespoons packed dark brown sugar

1 medium onion, finely chopped

3 cups vegetable broth

3 tablespoons tomato paste

¼ teaspoon ground allspice

1 can (5 ounces) evaporated milk

¼ cup shredded fresh basil (about 10 large leaves)

Salt and black pepper

Sprigs fresh basil (optional)

1. Preheat oven to 450°F. Line baking sheet with foil; spray with nonstick cooking spray. Arrange tomatoes on foil in single layer. Sprinkle with brown sugar; top with onion. Bake 25 minutes or until tomatoes look dry and light brown. Let tomatoes cool slightly; finely chop.

2. Place tomato mixture, 3 cups reserved liquid from tomatoes, broth, tomato paste and allspice in **CROCK-POT**® slow cooker; stir to blend. Cover; cook on LOW 8 hours or on HIGH 4 hours.

3. Add evaporated milk and shredded basil; season with salt and pepper. Cover; cook on HIGH 30 minutes or until heated through. Garnish each serving with basil sprig.

FRENCH ONION SOUP

Makes 8 servings

¼ cup (½ stick) butter

3 pounds yellow onions, sliced

1 tablespoon sugar

2 to 3 tablespoons dry white wine

8 cups beef broth

8 to 16 slices French bread

1 cup (4 ounces) shredded Gruyère or Swiss cheese

1. Melt butter in large skillet over medium-low heat. Add onions; cover and cook 10 minutes or just until onions are tender and transparent, but not browned.

2. Remove cover. Sprinkle sugar over onions; cook and stir 8 to 10 minutes or until onions are caramelized. Add wine to skillet; bring to a boil, scraping up any browned bits from bottom of skillet. Add to **CROCK-POT**® slow cooker. Stir in broth. Cover; cook on LOW 8 hours or on HIGH 6 hours.

3. Preheat broiler. To serve, ladle soup into individual soup bowls. Top each with 1 or 2 bread slices and cheese. Place under broiler until cheese is melted and bubbly.

VARIATION: Substitute 1 cup dry white wine for 1 cup of beef broth.

ITALIAN SAUSAGE SOUP

Makes 4 to 6 servings

- 1 pound mild Italian sausage, casings removed
- ½ cup dry bread crumbs
- ¼ cup grated Parmesan cheese, plus additional for garnish
- ¼ cup milk
- 1 egg
- ½ teaspoon dried basil
- ½ teaspoon black pepper
- ¼ teaspoon garlic salt
- 4 cups hot chicken broth
- 1 tablespoon tomato paste
- 1 clove garlic, minced
- ¼ teaspoon red pepper flakes
- ½ cup uncooked mini pasta shells*
- 1 bag (10 ounces) baby spinach leaves

*Or use other tiny pasta, such as ditalini (mini tubes) or farfallini (mini bowties).

1. Combine sausage, bread crumbs, ¼ cup cheese, milk, egg, basil, black pepper and garlic salt in large bowl; shape into ½-inch balls.

2. Combine broth, tomato paste, garlic and red pepper flakes in **CROCK-POT®** slow cooker; stir to blend. Add meatballs. Cover; cook on LOW 5 to 6 hours.

3. Add pasta. Cover; cook on LOW 30 minutes. Stir in spinach when pasta is tender. Ladle into bowls; sprinkle with additional cheese.

CELERY-LEEK BISQUE

Makes 4 to 6 servings

3 bunches leeks (about 3 pounds), trimmed and well rinsed

2 medium stalks celery, sliced

1 medium carrot, sliced

3 cloves garlic, minced

2 cans (about 14 ounces *each*) vegetable broth

1 package (8 ounces) cream cheese with garlic and herbs

2 cups half-and-half, plus additional for garnish

Salt and black pepper

Fresh basil leaves (optional)

1. Combine leeks, celery, carrot, garlic and broth in **CROCK-POT**® slow cooker; stir to blend. Cover; cook on LOW 8 hours or on HIGH 4 hours.

2. Pour mixture, 1 cup at a time, into food processor or blender; process until smooth. Return batches to **CROCK-POT**® slow cooker. Add cream cheese to last batch; purée until smooth. Stir cream cheese mixture and 2 cups half-and-half into soup. Season with salt and pepper. Garnish with additional half-and-half and basil leaves.

TIP | It's very important to rinse leeks thoroughly before using. The gritty sand in which leeks are grown can become trapped between the layers of leaves and can be difficult to see. Cut trimmed leeks in half lengthwise and submerge in several inches of cool water several times to rinse off any trapped sand.

VEGETABLE SOUP WITH BEANS

Makes 4 servings

4 cups vegetable broth

1 can (about 15 ounces) cannellini beans, rinsed and drained

1 can (about 14 ounces) diced tomatoes

16 baby carrots

1 medium onion, chopped

1 ounce dried oyster mushrooms, chopped

3 tablespoons tomato paste

2 teaspoons garlic powder

1 teaspoon dried basil

1 teaspoon dried oregano

½ teaspoon dried rosemary

½ teaspoon dried marjoram

½ teaspoon dried sage

½ teaspoon dried thyme

¼ teaspoon black pepper

French bread slices, toasted (optional)

Combine broth, beans, tomatoes, carrots, onion, mushrooms, tomato paste, garlic powder, basil, oregano, rosemary, marjoram, sage, thyme and pepper in **CROCK-POT**® slow cooker; stir to blend. Cover; cook on LOW 8 hours or on HIGH 4 to 5 hours. Serve with bread, if desired.

BLACK BEAN CHIPOTLE SOUP

Makes 4 to 6 servings

1 pound dried black beans, rinsed and sorted

6 cups chicken or vegetable broth

1 large onion, chopped

1 cup crushed tomatoes

2 stalks celery, diced

2 carrots, diced

1 can (4 ounces) diced mild green chiles, drained

2 canned chipotle peppers in adobo sauce, chopped

2 teaspoons ground cumin

Salt and black pepper

Optional toppings: sour cream, sausage, salsa, chopped fresh cilantro

1. Place beans in large bowl; cover completely with water. Soak 6 to 8 hours or overnight.* Drain beans; discard water.

2. Place beans in **CROCK-POT**® slow cooker. Add broth, onion, tomatoes, celery, carrots, chiles, chipotle peppers and cumin; stir to blend.

3. Cover; cook on LOW 7 to 8 hours or on HIGH 4½ to 5 hours. Season with salt and black pepper. Place mixture in batches in food processor or blender; process to desired consistency. Top as desired.

*To quick soak beans, place beans in large saucepan. Cover with water; bring to a boil over high heat. Boil 2 minutes. Remove from heat; let soak, covered, 1 hour.

FISH STOCK

Makes about 8 cups

2 tablespoons olive oil
1 large onion, chopped
2 carrots, chopped
2 stalks celery, chopped
1 cup dry white wine
2 whole tilapia fillets, scaled and gutted

8 cups water
1 sprig fresh thyme
4 sprigs fresh Italian parsley
4 whole black peppercorns
2 teaspoons salt

1. Heat oil in skillet over medium-high heat. Add onion, carrots and celery; cook 6 to 8 minutes or until tender and lightly browned. Add wine, stirring to scrape up any browned bits from bottom of skillet. Pour mixture into **CROCK-POT**® slow cooker. Stir in water, tilapia, thyme, parsley, peppercorns and salt. Cover; cook on HIGH 3½ hours.

2. Strain stock and discard solids. Allow stock to cool to room temperature; place in refrigerator overnight. Discard any fat that rises to top of chilled stock before using or freezing.

NOTE: To quickly cool down stock, place stockpot in a sink or large bowl of ice, stirring often.

EASY CORN CHOWDER

Makes 6 servings

2 cans (about 14 ounces *each*) chicken broth

1 bag (16 ounces) frozen corn, thawed

3 small red potatoes, cut into ½-inch pieces

1 red bell pepper, diced

1 medium onion, diced

1 stalk celery, sliced

½ teaspoon salt

½ teaspoon black pepper

¼ teaspoon ground coriander

½ cup whipping cream

8 slices bacon, crisp-cooked and crumbled

1. Place broth, corn, potatoes, bell pepper, onion, celery, salt, black pepper and coriander in **CROCK-POT**® slow cooker; stir to blend. Cover; cook on LOW 7 to 8 hours.

2. Partially mash soup mixture with potato masher to thicken. Turn **CROCK-POT**® slow cooker to HIGH. Stir in cream; cook on HIGH, uncovered, until heated through. Sprinkle with bacon.

SEAFOOD BOUILLABAISSE

Makes 4 servings

Nonstick cooking spray

½ bulb fennel, chopped

1 medium onion, chopped

2 cloves garlic, minced

1 can (28 ounces) tomato purée

2 cans (12 ounces *each*) beer

2 cups water

8 ounces clam juice

1 whole bay leaf

½ teaspoon salt

¼ teaspoon black pepper

½ pound red snapper, cut into 1-inch pieces

8 mussels, scrubbed and debearded

8 cherrystone clams

8 large raw shrimp, unpeeled and rinsed (with tails on)

4 lemon wedges

1. Spray large skillet with cooking spray; heat over medium-high heat. Add fennel, onion and garlic; cook and stir 5 minutes or until onion is soft and translucent. Remove fennel mixture to **CROCK-POT**® slow cooker. Add tomato purée, beer, water, clam juice, bay leaf, salt and pepper to **CROCK-POT**® slow cooker. Cover; cook on LOW 6 to 8 hours or on HIGH 3 to 4 hours.

2. Add fish, mussels, clams and shrimp to **CROCK-POT**® slow cooker. Cover; cook on LOW 15 minutes or until fish flakes when tested with fork. Discard any mussels and clams that do not open.

3. Remove and discard bay leaf. Ladle broth into wide soup bowls; top with fish, mussels, clams and shrimp. Squeeze lemon over each serving.

CHILIES

VEGETARIAN CHILI

Makes 4 servings

1 tablespoon vegetable oil

1 cup chopped onion

1 cup chopped red bell pepper

2 tablespoons minced jalapeño pepper*

1 clove garlic, minced

1 can (about 28 ounces) stewed tomatoes

1 can (about 15 ounces) black beans, rinsed and drained

1 can (about 15 ounces) chickpeas, rinsed and drained

½ cup frozen corn

¼ cup tomato paste

1 teaspoon sugar

1 teaspoon ground cumin

1 teaspoon dried basil

1 teaspoon chili powder

¼ teaspoon black pepper

*Jalapeño peppers can sting and irritate the skin, so wear rubber gloves when handling peppers and do not touch your eyes.

1. Heat oil in large skillet over medium-high heat. Add onion, bell pepper, jalapeño pepper and garlic; cook and stir 5 minutes or until vegetables are softened. Remove onion mixture to **CROCK-POT**® slow cooker using slotted spoon.

2. Add tomatoes, beans, chickpeas, corn, tomato paste, sugar, cumin, basil, chili powder and black pepper to **CROCK-POT**® slow cooker; stir to blend. Cover; cook on LOW 4 to 5 hours.

SIMPLE BEEF CHILI

Makes 8 servings

3 pounds ground beef

2 cans (about 14 ounces *each*) unsalted diced tomatoes

2 cans (about 15 ounces *each*) kidney beans, rinsed and drained

2 cups chopped onions

1 package (10 ounces) frozen corn

1 cup chopped green bell pepper

1 can (8 ounces) tomato sauce

3 tablespoons chili powder

1 teaspoon garlic powder

½ teaspoon ground cumin

½ teaspoon dried oregano

Prepared corn bread (optional)

1. Brown beef in large skillet over medium-high heat 6 to 8 minutes, stirring to break up meat. Remove to **CROCK-POT**® slow cooker using slotted spoon.

2. Add tomatoes, beans, onions, corn, bell pepper, tomato sauce, chili powder, garlic powder, cumin and oregano to **CROCK-POT**® slow cooker. Cover; cook on LOW 4 hours. Serve with corn bread, if desired.

TIP | The flavor and aroma of herbs and spices may lessen during a longer cooking time. So, when slow cooking in your **CROCK-POT**® slow cooker, be sure to taste and adjust seasonings before serving.

KICK'N CHILI

Makes 6 servings

2 pounds ground beef

2 cloves garlic, minced

1 tablespoon *each* salt, ground cumin, chili powder, paprika, dried oregano and black pepper

2 teaspoons red pepper flakes

¼ teaspoon ground red pepper

1 tablespoon vegetable oil

3 cans (about 14 ounces *each*) diced tomatoes with mild green chiles

1 jar (16 ounces) salsa

1 onion, chopped

1. Combine beef, garlic, salt, cumin, chili powder, paprika, oregano, black pepper, red pepper flakes and ground red pepper in large bowl.

2. Heat oil in large skillet over medium-high heat. Brown beef 6 to 8 minutes, stirring to break up meat. Drain fat. Add tomatoes, salsa and onion; mix well. Remove to **CROCK-POT**® slow cooker. Cover; cook on LOW 4 to 6 hours.

TIP | This chunky chili is perfect for the spicy food lover in your family. Reduce the red pepper flakes for a milder flavor.

BLACK AND WHITE CHILI

Makes 6 servings

Nonstick cooking spray

1 pound boneless, skinless chicken breasts, cut into ¾-inch pieces

1 cup chopped onion

1 can (about 15 ounces) Great Northern beans, rinsed and drained

1 can (about 15 ounces) black beans, rinsed and drained

1 can (about 14 ounces) stewed tomatoes

2 tablespoons Texas-style chili seasoning mix

1. Spray large skillet with cooking spray; heat over medium heat. Add chicken and onion; cook and stir 5 minutes or until chicken is browned.

2. Add chicken mixture, beans, tomatoes and chili seasoning mix to **CROCK-POT®** slow cooker; stir to blend. Cover; cook on LOW 4 to 4½ hours.

SERVING SUGGESTION: For a change of pace, this delicious chili is excellent served over cooked rice or pasta.

HEARTY PORK AND BACON CHILI

Makes 8 to 10 servings

2½ pounds pork shoulder, cut into 1-inch pieces

3½ teaspoons salt, divided

1¼ teaspoons black pepper, divided

1 tablespoon vegetable oil

4 slices thick-cut bacon, diced

2 medium onions, chopped

1 red bell pepper, chopped

¼ cup chili powder

2 tablespoons tomato paste

1 tablespoon minced garlic

1 tablespoon ground cumin

1 tablespoon smoked paprika

1 bottle (12 ounces) pale ale

2 cans (about 14 ounces *each*) diced tomatoes

2 cups water

¾ cup dried kidney beans, rinsed and sorted

¾ cup dried black beans, rinsed and sorted

3 tablespoons cornmeal

Feta cheese and chopped fresh cilantro (optional)

1. Season pork with 1 teaspoon salt and 1 teaspoon black pepper. Heat oil in large skillet over medium-high heat. Cook pork in batches 6 minutes or until browned on all sides. Remove to **CROCK-POT®** slow cooker using slotted spoon.

2. Heat same skillet over medium heat. Add bacon; cook and stir until crisp. Remove to **CROCK-POT®** slow cooker using slotted spoon.

3. Pour off all but 2 tablespoons fat from skillet. Return skillet to medium heat. Add onions and bell pepper; cook and stir 6 minutes or just until softened. Stir in chili powder, tomato paste, garlic, cumin, paprika, remaining 2½ teaspoons salt and remaining ¼ teaspoon black pepper; cook and stir 1 minute. Stir in ale. Bring to a simmer, scraping up any browned bits from bottom of skillet. Pour over pork in **CROCK-POT®** slow cooker. Stir in tomatoes, water, beans and cornmeal.

4. Cover; cook on LOW 10 hours. Turn off heat. Let stand 10 minutes. Skim fat from surface. Garnish each serving with cheese and cilantro.

BEEF CHUCK CHILI

Makes 8 to 10 servings

½ cup plus 2 tablespoons olive oil, divided

1 boneless beef chuck roast (5 pounds), trimmed*

3 cups finely chopped onions

2 green bell peppers, chopped

4 poblano peppers, seeded and finely chopped**

2 serrano peppers, seeded and minced**

3 jalapeño peppers, seeded and minced**

2 tablespoons minced garlic

1 can (28 ounces) crushed tomatoes, undrained

½ cup Mexican lager

¼ cup hot pepper sauce

1 tablespoon ground cumin

Prepared corn bread

*Unless you have a 5-, 6- or 7-quart CROCK-POT® slow cooker, cut any roast larger than 2½ pounds in half so it cooks completely.

**Poblano, serrano and jalapeño peppers can sting and irritate the skin. Wear rubber gloves when handling peppers and do not touch your eyes.

1. Heat ½ cup oil in large skillet over medium-high heat. Add roast; brown on both sides. Remove to **CROCK-POT**® slow cooker.

2. Heat remaining 2 tablespoons oil in same skillet over low heat. Add onions, bell peppers, poblano peppers, serrano peppers, jalapeño peppers and garlic; cook and stir 7 minutes or until onions are tender. Remove to **CROCK-POT**® slow cooker. Stir in tomatoes. Cover; cook on LOW 4 to 5 hours.

3. Remove beef to large cutting board; shred with two forks. Add lager, hot pepper sauce and cumin to cooking liquid. Return beef to cooking liquid; mix well. Serve over corn bread.

CHICKEN AND BLACK BEAN CHILI

Makes 4 servings

1 pound boneless, skinless chicken thighs, cut into 1-inch pieces

2 teaspoons chili powder

2 teaspoons ground cumin

¾ teaspoon salt

1 green bell pepper, diced

1 small onion, chopped

3 cloves garlic, minced

1 can (about 14 ounces) diced tomatoes

1 cup chunky salsa

1 can (about 15 ounces) black beans, rinsed and drained

Optional toppings: sour cream, diced tomatoes, shredded Cheddar cheese, sprigs fresh cilantro and/or tortilla chips

1. Combine chicken, chili powder, cumin and salt in **CROCK-POT**® slow cooker; toss to coat.

2. Add bell pepper, onion and garlic; mix well. Stir in tomatoes and salsa. Cover; cook on LOW 5 to 6 hours or on HIGH 2½ to 3 hours.

3. Stir in beans. Cover; cook on HIGH 5 to 10 minutes or until heated through. Ladle into shallow bowls; serve with desired toppings.

CINCINNATI CHILI

Makes 6 servings

1 tablespoon vegetable oil

2 onions, chopped

2 pounds ground beef

1 can (28 ounces) diced tomatoes

1 cup tomato sauce

½ cup water

3 cloves garlic, minced

1 tablespoon unsweetened cocoa powder

1 tablespoon chili powder

2½ teaspoons ground cinnamon

2 teaspoons salt

1½ teaspoons ground cumin

1½ teaspoons Worcestershire sauce

1¼ teaspoons ground allspice

¾ teaspoon ground red pepper

12 ounces cooked spaghetti

Optional toppings: chopped onions, shredded Cheddar cheese, kidney beans and/or oyster crackers

1. Heat oil in large skillet over medium-high heat. Add onions; cook 2 to 3 minutes or until translucent. Add beef; cook until beef is browned, stirring to break up meat. Drain fat. Remove beef mixture to **CROCK-POT**® slow cooker using slotted spoon.

2. Stir tomatoes, tomato sauce, water, garlic, cocoa, chili powder, cinnamon, salt, cumin, Worcestershire sauce, allspice and ground red pepper into **CROCK-POT**® slow cooker. Cover; cook on LOW 7 to 8 hours or on HIGH 3½ to 4 hours. Spoon chili over spaghetti. Top as desired.

WHITE CHICKEN CHILI

Makes 6 to 8 servings

8 ounces dried navy beans, rinsed and sorted

1 tablespoon vegetable oil

2 pounds boneless, skinless chicken breasts (about 4)

2 onions, chopped

1 tablespoon minced garlic

2 teaspoons ground cumin

2 teaspoons salt

1 teaspoon dried oregano

¼ teaspoon black pepper

¼ teaspoon ground red pepper (optional)

4 cups chicken broth

1 can (4 ounces) fire-roasted diced mild green chiles, rinsed and drained

¼ cup chopped fresh cilantro

1. Place beans on bottom of **CROCK-POT**® slow cooker. Heat oil in large skillet over medium-high heat. Add chicken; cook 8 minutes or until browned on all sides. Remove to **CROCK-POT**® slow cooker.

2. Heat same skillet over medium heat. Add onions; cook 6 minutes or until softened and lightly browned. Add garlic, cumin, salt, oregano, black pepper and ground red pepper, if desired; cook and stir 1 minute. Add broth and chiles; bring to a simmer, stirring to scrape up any browned bits from bottom of skillet. Remove onion mixture to **CROCK-POT**® slow cooker.

3. Cover; cook on LOW 5 hours. Remove chicken to large cutting board; shred with two forks. Return chicken to **CROCK-POT**® slow cooker. Stir in cilantro.

SAVORY CHICKEN AND OREGANO CHILI

Makes 8 servings

3 cans (about 15 ounces *each*) Great Northern or cannellini beans, rinsed and drained

3½ cups chicken broth

2 cups chopped cooked chicken breasts

2 red bell peppers, chopped

1 onion, chopped

1 can (4 ounces) diced mild green chiles, drained

3 cloves garlic, minced

2 teaspoons ground cumin

1 teaspoon salt

1 tablespoon minced fresh oregano

1. Combine beans, broth, chicken, bell peppers, onion, chiles, garlic, cumin and salt in **CROCK-POT**® slow cooker; stir to blend. Cover; cook on LOW 8 to 10 hours or on HIGH 4 to 5 hours.

2. Stir in oregano just before serving.

BEST EVER CHILI

Makes 8 servings

1½ **pounds ground beef**

1 **cup chopped onion**

2 **cans (about 15 ounces** *each***) kidney beans, drained and liquid reserved**

1½ **pounds plum tomatoes, diced**

1 **can (15 ounces) tomato paste**

3 **to 6 tablespoons chili powder**

Sour cream and chopped green onion (optional)

1. Brown beef and onion in large skillet 6 to 8 minutes over medium-high heat, stirring to break up meat. Drain fat. Remove beef mixture to **CROCK-POT**® slow cooker using slotted spoon.

2. Add beans, tomatoes, tomato paste, 1 cup reserved bean liquid and chili powder to **CROCK-POT**® slow cooker; mix well. Cover; cook on LOW 10 to 12 hours. Top each serving with sour cream and green onions, if desired.

THREE-BEAN CHILI WITH CHORIZO

Makes 6 to 8 servings

2 Mexican chorizo sausages (about 6 ounces *each*), casings removed

1 tablespoon vegetable oil

1 large onion, chopped

1 tablespoon salt

1 tablespoon tomato paste

1 tablespoon minced garlic

1 tablespoon chili powder

1 tablespoon ancho chili powder

2 to 3 teaspoons chipotle chili powder

2 teaspoons ground cumin

1 teaspoon ground coriander

3 cups water

2 cans (about 14 ounces *each*) crushed tomatoes

½ cup dried pinto beans, rinsed and sorted

½ cup dried kidney beans, rinsed and sorted

½ cup dried black beans, rinsed and sorted

Chopped fresh cilantro (optional)

1. Heat large nonstick skillet over medium-high heat. Add sausages; cook 3 to 4 minutes, stirring to break up meat. Remove to **CROCK-POT**® slow cooker using slotted spoon.

2. Wipe out skillet. Heat oil in same skillet over medium heat. Add onion; cook and stir 6 minutes or until softened. Add salt, tomato paste, garlic, chili powders, cumin and coriander; cook and stir 1 minute. Remove to **CROCK-POT**® slow cooker. Stir in water, tomatoes and beans.

3. Cover; cook on LOW 10 hours. Garnish each serving with cilantro.

NOTE: For spicier chili, use 1 tablespoon chipotle chili powder.

CHIPOTLE VEGETABLE CHILI WITH CHOCOLATE

Makes 6 servings

2 tablespoons olive oil

1 medium onion, chopped

1 medium green bell pepper, chopped

1 medium red bell pepper, chopped

1 cup frozen corn

1 can (28 ounces) diced tomatoes

1 can (about 15 ounces) black beans, rinsed and drained

1 can (about 15 ounces) pinto beans, rinsed and drained

1 tablespoon chili powder

1 teaspoon ground cumin

½ teaspoon chipotle chili powder

1 ounce semisweet chocolate, chopped

1. Heat oil in large skillet over medium-high heat. Add onion and bell peppers; cook and stir 4 minutes or until softened. Stir in corn; cook 3 minutes. Remove to **CROCK-POT**® slow cooker.

2. Stir tomatoes, beans, chili powder, cumin and chipotle chili powder into **CROCK-POT**® slow cooker. Cover; cook on LOW 6 to 7 hours. Stir chocolate into **CROCK-POT**® slow cooker until melted.

CLASSIC CHILI

Makes 6 servings

1½ pounds ground beef

1½ cups chopped onion

1 cup chopped green bell pepper

2 cloves garlic, minced

3 cans (about 15 ounces *each*) dark red kidney beans, rinsed and drained

2 cans (about 15 ounces *each*) tomato sauce

1 can (about 14 ounces) diced tomatoes

2 to 3 teaspoons chili powder

1 to 2 teaspoons ground mustard

¾ teaspoon dried basil

½ teaspoon black pepper

1 to 2 dried red chiles (optional)

Sprigs fresh cilantro (optional)

1. Brown beef, onion, bell pepper and garlic in large skillet over medium-high heat 6 to 8 minutes, stirring to break up meat. Remove beef mixture to **CROCK-POT®** slow cooker using slotted spoon.

2. Add beans, tomato sauce, tomatoes, chili powder, mustard, basil, black pepper and chiles, if desired, to **CROCK-POT®** slow cooker; stir to blend. Cover; cook on LOW 8 to 10 hours or on HIGH 4 to 5 hours. If used, remove chiles before serving. Garnish with cilantro.

THREE-BEAN CHIPOTLE CHILI

Makes 6 servings

2 tablespoons olive oil

1 onion, chopped

1 green bell pepper, chopped

2 cloves garlic, minced

2 cans (about 15 ounces *each*) pinto or pink beans, rinsed and drained

1 can (about 15 ounces) small white beans, rinsed and drained

1 can (about 15 ounces) chickpeas, rinsed and drained

1 cup frozen or canned corn

1 cup water

1 can (6 ounces) tomato paste

1 or 2 canned chipotle peppers in adobo sauce, finely chopped

Salt and black pepper

Sour cream and shredded Cheddar cheese (optional)

1. Heat oil in large skillet over medium heat. Add onion, bell pepper and garlic; cook and stir until softened. Remove to **CROCK-POT®** slow cooker.

2. Add beans, chickpeas, corn, water, tomato paste and chipotle peppers to **CROCK-POT®** slow cooker. Season with salt and black pepper; stir to blend. Cover; cook on LOW 3½ to 4 hours. Top with sour cream and cheese.

THREE-BEAN TURKEY CHILI

Makes 6 to 8 servings

1 pound ground turkey

1 small onion, chopped

1 can (28 ounces) diced tomatoes

1 can (about 15 ounces) chickpeas, rinsed and drained

1 can (about 15 ounces) kidney beans, rinsed and drained

1 can (about 15 ounces) black beans, rinsed and drained

1 can (8 ounces) tomato sauce

1 can (4 ounces) diced mild green chiles

1 to 2 tablespoons chili powder

1. Place turkey and onion in large skillet over medium-high heat; cook and stir 6 to 8 minutes or until turkey is browned. Drain fat. Remove to **CROCK-POT®** slow cooker.

2. Add tomatoes, chickpeas, beans, tomato sauce, chiles and chili powder to **CROCK-POT®** slow cooker; mix well. Cover; cook on HIGH 6 to 8 hours.

BLACK BEAN MUSHROOM CHILI

Makes 4 servings

1 tablespoon vegetable oil

2 cups (8 ounces) sliced baby
   bella or button mushrooms

1 cup chopped onion

4 cloves garlic, minced

1 can (about 15 ounces) black
   beans, rinsed and drained

1 can (about 14 ounces) fire-
   roasted diced tomatoes

1 cup salsa

1 yellow or green bell pepper,
   finely diced

2 teaspoons chili powder or
   ground cumin

Sour cream (optional)

1. Coat inside of **CROCK-POT**® slow cooker with nonstick cooking spray. Heat oil in large skillet over medium heat. Add mushrooms, onion and garlic; cook 8 minutes or until mushrooms have released their liquid and liquid has thickened slightly.

2. Combine mushroom mixture, beans, tomatoes, salsa, bell pepper and chili powder in **CROCK-POT**® slow cooker; stir to blend. Cover; cook on LOW 5 to 6 hours or on HIGH 2½ to 3 hours. Ladle into shallow bowls. Top with sour cream, if desired.

MAMA'S BEER CHILI

Makes 4 to 6 servings

1 can (28 ounces) crushed tomatoes

1 package (10 ounces) frozen corn

1 can (about 15 ounces) kidney beans, rinsed and drained

1 cup beer (preferably dark)

⅓ cup honey

⅓ cup diced mild green chiles

3 tablespoons chili powder

3 tablespoons hot pepper sauce

3 cubes beef bouillon

1 to 2 tablespoons all-purpose flour

1 teaspoon curry powder

2 tablespoons olive oil

1 large onion (preferably Vidalia), diced

4 cloves garlic, crushed

1½ to 2 pounds ground turkey

Sliced green onions (optional)

1. Combine tomatoes, corn, beans, beer, honey, chiles, chili powder, hot pepper sauce, bouillon cubes, flour and curry powder in **CROCK-POT®** slow cooker; stir to blend.

2. Heat oil in large skillet over medium-low heat. Add diced onion; cook and stir 5 minutes. Add garlic; cook and stir 2 minutes. Add turkey; cook and stir 6 to 8 minutes or until turkey is no longer pink. Remove to **CROCK-POT®** slow cooker.

3. Cover; cook on LOW 8 to 10 hours or on HIGH 4 to 6 hours. Garnish each serving with green onions.

PORK TENDERLOIN CHILI

Makes 8 servings

1½ to 2 pounds pork tenderloin, cooked and cut into 2-inch pieces

2 cans (about 15 ounces *each*) pinto beans, rinsed and drained

2 cans (about 15 ounces *each*) black beans, rinsed and drained

2 cans (about 14 ounces *each*) whole tomatoes

2 cans (4 ounces *each*) diced mild green chiles

1 package (1¼ ounces) taco seasoning mix

Diced avocado (optional)

Combine pork, beans, tomatoes, chiles and taco seasoning mix in **CROCK-POT®** slow cooker; stir to blend. Cover; cook on LOW 4 hours. Top with avocado, if desired.

STEWS

COD FISH STEW

Makes 6 to 8 servings

½ pound bacon, coarsely chopped

1 large carrot, diced

1 large onion, diced

2 stalks celery, diced

2 cloves garlic, minced

Salt and black pepper

3 cups water

2 cups clam juice or fish broth

1 can (28 ounces) plum tomatoes, drained

2 potatoes, diced

½ cup dry white wine

3 tablespoons chopped fresh Italian parsley

3 tablespoons tomato paste

3 saffron threads

2½ pounds fresh cod, skinned and cut into 1-inch pieces

1. Heat medium skillet over medium heat. Add bacon; cook and stir until crisp. Add carrot, onion, celery and garlic to skillet; season with salt and pepper. Cook and stir 6 to 8 minutes or until vegetables are softened.

2. Remove bacon and vegetables to **CROCK-POT**® slow cooker. Stir in water, clam juice, tomatoes, potatoes, wine, parsley, tomato paste and saffron. Cover; cook on LOW 6 to 7 hours or on HIGH 3 to 4 hours.

3. Add cod. Cover; cook on HIGH 10 to 20 minutes or until cod is just cooked through.

NOTE: Cod is a great fish to use for a soup or stew. The thick creamy white fish becomes a hearty meal when paired with bacon and tomato.

CURRIED VEGETABLE AND CASHEW STEW

Makes 8 servings

1 medium potato, cut into ½-inch cubes

1 can (about 15 ounces) chickpeas, rinsed and drained

1 can (about 14 ounces) diced tomatoes

1 medium (about ½ pound) eggplant, cut into ½-inch cubes

1 medium onion, chopped

1 cup vegetable broth

2 tablespoons quick-cooking tapioca

2 teaspoons grated fresh ginger

2 teaspoons curry powder

½ teaspoon salt

¼ teaspoon black pepper

1 medium zucchini (about 8 ounces), cut into ½-inch cubes

2 tablespoons golden raisins

½ cup frozen peas

½ cup cashew nuts

1. Combine potato, chickpeas, tomatoes, eggplant, onion, broth, tapioca, ginger, curry powder, salt and pepper in **CROCK-POT**® slow cooker; stir to blend. Cover; cook on LOW 8 to 9 hours.

2. Stir zucchini, raisins, peas and cashews into **CROCK-POT**® slow cooker. Turn **CROCK-POT**® slow cooker to HIGH. Cover; cook on HIGH 1 hour or until zucchini is tender.

CHICKEN AND MUSHROOM STEW

Makes 6 servings

4 tablespoons vegetable oil, divided

2 medium leeks (white and light green parts only), halved lengthwise and thinly sliced crosswise

1 carrot, cut into 1-inch pieces

1 stalk celery, diced

6 boneless, skinless chicken thighs (about 2 pounds)

Salt and black pepper

12 ounces cremini mushrooms, quartered

¼ cup all-purpose flour

1 ounce dried porcini mushrooms, rehydrated in 1½ cups hot water and chopped, soaking liquid strained and reserved

1 teaspoon minced garlic

1 sprig fresh thyme

1 whole bay leaf

½ cup dry white wine

1 cup chicken broth

1. Heat 1 tablespoon oil in large skillet over medium heat. Add leeks; cook 8 minutes or until softened. Remove to **CROCK-POT**® slow cooker. Add carrot and celery.

2. Heat 1 tablespoon oil in same skillet over medium-high heat. Season chicken with salt and pepper. Add chicken in batches; cook 8 minutes or until browned on both sides. Remove to **CROCK-POT**® slow cooker.

3. Heat remaining 2 tablespoons oil in same skillet. Add cremini mushrooms; cook 7 minutes or until mushrooms have released their liquid and started to brown. Add flour, porcini mushrooms, garlic, thyme and bay leaf; cook and stir 1 minute. Add wine; cook and stir until evaporated, stirring to scrape up any browned bits from bottom of skillet. Add reserved soaking liquid and broth; bring to a simmer. Pour mixture into **CROCK-POT**® slow cooker.

4. Cover; cook on HIGH 2 to 3 hours. Remove and discard thyme sprig and bay leaf before serving.

CAJUN PORK SAUSAGE AND SHRIMP STEW

Makes 6 servings

1 can (28 ounces) diced tomatoes

1 package (16 ounces) frozen mixed vegetables (potatoes, carrots, celery and onions)

1 package (14 to 16 ounces) kielbasa or smoked sausage, cut diagonally into ¾-inch slices

2 teaspoons Cajun seasoning

¾ pound large raw shrimp, peeled and deveined (with tails on)

2 cups (8 ounces) frozen sliced okra, thawed

Hot cooked rice or grits

1. Coat inside of **CROCK-POT**® slow cooker with nonstick cooking spray. Combine tomatoes, vegetables, sausage and Cajun seasoning in **CROCK-POT**® slow cooker; stir to blend. Cover; cook on LOW 5 to 6 hours or on HIGH 2 to 2½ hours.

2. Stir shrimp and okra into **CROCK-POT**® slow cooker. Cover; cook on HIGH 30 to 35 minutes or until shrimp are pink and opaque. Serve over rice.

ITALIAN STEW

Makes 4 servings

1 can (about 14 ounces) chicken broth

1 can (about 14 ounces) Italian stewed tomatoes with peppers and onions, undrained

1 package (9 ounces) fully cooked spicy chicken sausage, sliced

2 small zucchini, sliced

2 carrots, thinly sliced

1 can (about 15 ounces) Great Northern, cannellini or navy beans, rinsed and drained

2 tablespoons chopped fresh basil (optional)

1. Combine broth, tomatoes, sausage, zucchini and carrots in **CROCK-POT®** slow cooker; stir to blend. Cover; cook on LOW 6 to 7 hours or on HIGH 3 to 4 hours.

2. Stir in beans. Cover; cook on HIGH 10 to 15 minutes or until beans are heated through. Ladle into shallow bowls. Garnish with basil.

CARIBBEAN CHICKEN STEW

Makes 4 servings

2 boneless, skinless chicken breasts (½ pound *total*)

1¼ teaspoons salt, divided

1 teaspoon ground cumin, divided

1 teaspoon dried thyme, divided

1 teaspoon black pepper, divided

½ teaspoon allspice, divided

1 tablespoon extra virgin olive oil

1 can (13½ ounces) unsweetened coconut milk

1½ cups chicken broth

1 cup onion, chopped

1 jalapeño pepper, seeded and minced*

2 cloves garlic, minced

1 whole bay leaf

2 sweet potatoes, cubed

1 can (about 15 ounces) chickpeas, rinsed and drained

⅓ cup chopped fresh cilantro

Juice of 1 medium lime

Jalapeño peppers can sting and irritate the skin, so wear rubber gloves when handling peppers and do not touch your eyes.

1. Season chicken with ½ teaspoon salt, ½ teaspoon cumin, ½ teaspoon thyme, ½ teaspoon black pepper and ¼ teaspoon allspice. Heat oil in medium skillet over medium-high heat. Add chicken; brown 2 minutes on each side. Remove chicken to **CROCK-POT®** slow cooker.

2. Add coconut milk, broth, onion, jalapeño pepper, garlic, remaining ¾ teaspoon salt, ½ teaspoon cumin, ½ teaspoon thyme, ½ teaspoon black pepper, ¼ teaspoon allspice and bay leaf to **CROCK-POT®** slow cooker; stir to blend. Cover; cook on LOW 7 hours or on HIGH 3 hours.

3. Turn off heat. Remove chicken to large cutting board; shred with two forks. Let cooking liquid stand 5 minutes. Skim off and discard fat. Stir chicken, potatoes and chickpeas into **CROCK-POT®** slow cooker.

4. Cover; cook on LOW 1 hour or on HIGH 30 minutes. Remove and discard bay leaf. Add cilantro and lime juice just before serving.

LAMB AND CHICKPEA STEW

Makes 6 servings

1 pound lamb stew meat

2 teaspoons salt, divided

2 tablespoons vegetable oil, divided

1 large onion, chopped

1 tablespoon minced garlic

1½ teaspoons ground cumin

1 teaspoon ground turmeric

1 teaspoon ground coriander

1 teaspoon ground cinnamon

¼ teaspoon black pepper

2 cups chicken broth

1 cup diced canned tomatoes, drained

1 cup dried chickpeas, rinsed and sorted

½ cup chopped dried apricots

¼ cup chopped fresh Italian parsley

2 tablespoons honey

2 tablespoons lemon juice

Hot cooked couscous

1. Season lamb with 1 teaspoon salt. Heat 1 tablespoon oil in large skillet over medium-high heat. Add lamb; cook and stir 8 minutes or until browned on all sides. Remove to **CROCK-POT**® slow cooker.

2. Heat remaining 1 tablespoon oil in same skillet over medium heat. Add onion; cook and stir 6 minutes or until softened. Add garlic, remaining 1 teaspoon salt, cumin, turmeric, coriander, cinnamon and pepper; cook and stir 1 minute. Add broth and tomatoes; cook and stir 5 minutes, scraping up any brown bits from bottom of skillet. Remove to **CROCK-POT**® slow cooker. Stir in chickpeas.

3. Cover; cook on LOW 7 hours. Stir in apricots. Cover; cook on LOW 1 hour. Turn off heat. Let stand 10 minutes. Skim off and discard fat. Stir in parsley, honey and lemon juice. Serve over couscous.

CLASSIC BEEF STEW

Makes 8 servings

2½ pounds cubed beef stew meat

¼ cup all-purpose flour

2 tablespoons olive oil, divided

3 cups beef broth

16 baby carrots

8 fingerling potatoes, halved crosswise

1 medium onion, chopped

1 ounce dried oyster mushrooms, chopped

2 teaspoons garlic powder

1 teaspoon dried basil

1 teaspoon dried oregano

½ teaspoon dried rosemary

½ teaspoon dried marjoram

½ teaspoon dried sage

½ teaspoon dried thyme

Salt and black pepper (optional)

Chopped fresh Italian parsley (optional)

1. Combine beef and flour in large bowl; toss well to coat. Heat 1 tablespoon oil in large skillet over medium-high heat. Add half of beef; cook and stir 4 minutes or until browned. Remove to **CROCK-POT**® slow cooker. Repeat with remaining oil and beef.

2. Add broth, carrots, potatoes, onion, mushrooms, garlic powder, basil, oregano, rosemary, marjoram, sage and thyme to **CROCK-POT**® slow cooker; stir to blend. Cover; cook on LOW 10 to 12 hours or on HIGH 5 to 6 hours. Season with salt and pepper, if desired. Garnish with parsley.

EASY BEEF STEW

Makes 6 to 8 servings

1½ to 2 pounds cubed beef stew meat

4 medium potatoes, cubed

4 carrots, cut into 1½-inch pieces *or* 4 cups baby carrots

1 medium onion, cut into 8 slices

2 cans (8 ounces *each*) tomato sauce

1 teaspoon salt

½ teaspoon black pepper

Combine beef, potatoes, carrots, onion, tomato sauce, salt and pepper in **CROCK-POT**® slow cooker; stir to blend. Cover; cook on LOW 8 to 10 hours.

BUTTERNUT SQUASH, CHICKPEA AND LENTIL STEW

Makes 6 servings

2 cups peeled and diced butternut squash (½-inch pieces)

2 cups vegetable broth

1 can (about 15 ounces) chickpeas, rinsed and drained

1 can (about 14 ounces) fire-roasted diced tomatoes

1 cup chopped sweet onion

¾ cup dried brown lentils, rinsed and sorted

2 teaspoons ground cumin or coriander

¾ teaspoon salt

Olive oil (optional)

Sprigs fresh thyme (optional)

Coat inside of **CROCK-POT**® slow cooker with nonstick cooking spray. Combine squash, broth, chickpeas, tomatoes, onion, lentils, cumin and salt in **CROCK-POT**® slow cooker; stir to blend. Cover; cook on LOW 8 to 9 hours or on HIGH 4 to 4½ hours or until squash and lentils are tender. Ladle into shallow bowls. Drizzle with oil, if desired. Garnish with thyme.

ASIAN SWEET POTATO AND CORN STEW

Makes 6 servings

1 tablespoon vegetable oil

1 large onion, chopped

2 tablespoons peeled minced fresh ginger

½ jalapeño or serrano pepper, seeded and minced*

2 cloves garlic, minced

1 cup frozen corn

2 teaspoons curry powder

1 can (13½ ounces) unsweetened coconut milk

1 teaspoon cornstarch

4 sweet potatoes, cut into ¾-inch cubes

1 can (about 14 ounces) vegetable broth

1 tablespoon soy sauce

Hot cooked jasmine or long grain rice

Chopped fresh cilantro, peanuts and green onions (optional)

*Jalapeño and serrano peppers can sting and irritate the skin, so wear rubber gloves when handling peppers and do not touch your eyes.

1. Heat oil in large skillet over medium heat. Add onion, ginger, jalapeño pepper and garlic; cook and stir 5 minutes. Remove from heat. Stir in corn and curry powder.

2. Stir coconut milk into cornstarch in **CROCK-POT**® slow cooker. Stir in potatoes, broth and soy sauce; top with curried corn. Cover; cook on LOW 5 to 6 hours. Stir gently to smooth cooking liquid. Spoon over rice in bowls. Garnish with cilantro, peanuts and green onions.

HEARTY LENTIL STEW

Makes 6 servings

1 cup dried lentils, rinsed and sorted

1 package (16 ounces) frozen green beans

2 cups cauliflower florets

1 cup chopped onion

1 cup baby carrots, cut into halves crosswise

3 cups vegetable broth

2 teaspoons ground cumin

¾ teaspoon ground ginger

1 can (15 ounces) chunky tomato sauce with garlic and herbs

½ cup dry-roasted peanuts

1. Layer lentils, green beans, cauliflower, onion and carrots in **CROCK-POT®** slow cooker. Combine broth, cumin and ginger in large bowl; stir to blend. Pour over vegetables in **CROCK-POT®** slow cooker.

2. Cover; cook on LOW 9 to 11 hours. Stir in tomato sauce. Cover; cook on LOW 10 minutes or until heated through. Sprinkle each serving evenly with peanuts.

CARIBBEAN SWEET POTATO AND BEAN STEW

Makes 4 servings

2 medium sweet potatoes (about 1 pound), cut into 1-inch cubes

2 cups frozen cut green beans

1 can (about 15 ounces) black beans, rinsed and drained

1 can (about 14 ounces) vegetable broth

1 small onion, sliced

2 teaspoons Caribbean jerk seasoning

½ teaspoon dried thyme

¼ teaspoon salt

¼ teaspoon ground cinnamon

⅓ cup slivered almonds, toasted*

To toast almonds, spread in single layer in heavy skillet. Cook and stir over medium heat 1 to 2 minutes or until nuts are lightly browned.

Combine potatoes, beans, broth, onion, jerk seasoning, thyme, salt and cinnamon in **CROCK-POT®** slow cooker. Cover; cook on LOW 5 to 6 hours. Sprinkle each serving evenly with almonds.

SUMMER VEGETABLE STEW

Makes 4 servings

---

1 cup vegetable broth

1 can (about 15 ounces) chickpeas, rinsed and drained

1 medium zucchini, cut into ½-inch pieces

1 summer squash, cut into ½-inch pieces

4 large plum tomatoes, cut into ½-inch pieces

1 cup frozen corn

½ to 1 teaspoon dried rosemary

¼ cup grated Asiago or Parmesan cheese

1 tablespoon chopped fresh Italian parsley

Combine broth, chickpeas, zucchini, squash, tomatoes, corn and rosemary in **CROCK-POT®** slow cooker; stir to blend. Cover; cook on LOW 8 hours or on HIGH 5 hours. Top each serving evenly with cheese and parsley.

CHICKEN STEW WITH HERB DUMPLINGS

Makes 4 servings

2 cups sliced carrots

1 cup chopped onion

1 green bell pepper, sliced

½ cup sliced celery

2 cans (about 14 ounces *each*) chicken broth, divided

⅔ cup all-purpose flour

1 pound boneless, skinless chicken breasts, cut into 1-inch pieces

1 large red potato, unpeeled and cut into 1-inch pieces

6 ounces mushrooms, halved

¾ cup frozen peas

1¼ teaspoons dried basil, divided

1 teaspoon dried rosemary, divided

½ teaspoon dried tarragon, divided

¼ cup whipping cream

¾ to 1 teaspoon salt

¼ teaspoon black pepper

1 cup biscuit baking mix

⅓ cup milk

1. Combine carrots, onion, bell pepper, celery and all but 1 cup broth in **CROCK-POT®** slow cooker. Cover; cook on LOW 2 hours.

2. Stir remaining 1 cup broth into flour in small bowl until smooth; whisk into **CROCK-POT®** slow cooker. Add chicken, potato, mushrooms, peas, 1 teaspoon basil, ¾ teaspoon rosemary and ¼ teaspoon tarragon. Cover; cook on LOW 4 hours or until vegetables and chicken are tender. Stir in cream, salt and black pepper.

3. Combine baking mix, remaining ¼ teaspoon basil, ¼ teaspoon rosemary and ¼ teaspoon tarragon in small bowl. Stir in milk until soft dough forms. Add dumpling mixture to top of stew in four large spoonfuls.

4. Cover; cook on LOW 30 to 45 minutes or until dumplings are firm and toothpick inserted into center comes out clean. Serve in shallow bowls.

HEARTY MEATBALL STEW

Makes 6 to 8 servings

3 pounds ground beef or ground turkey

1 cup seasoned dry bread crumbs

4 eggs

½ cup milk

¼ cup grated Romano cheese

2 teaspoons salt

2 teaspoons garlic salt

2 teaspoons black pepper

2 tablespoons olive oil

2 cups water

2 cups beef broth

1 can (about 14 ounces) stewed tomatoes, undrained

1 can (12 ounces) tomato paste

1 cup chopped carrots

1 cup chopped onions

¼ cup chopped celery

1 tablespoon Italian seasoning

1. Combine beef, bread crumbs, eggs, milk, cheese, salt, garlic salt and pepper in large bowl. Shape into 2-inch-round meatballs. Heat oil in skillet over medium-high heat. Brown meatballs on all sides. Remove to **CROCK-POT**® slow cooker.

2. Add remaining ingredients. Cover; cook on LOW 4 to 6 hours or on HIGH 2 to 4 hours.

ASIAN BEEF STEW

Makes 6 servings

2 onions, cut into ¼-inch slices

1½ pounds boneless beef round steak, sliced thin across the grain

2 stalks celery, sliced

2 carrots, sliced

1 cup sliced mushrooms

1 cup orange juice

1 cup beef broth

⅓ cup hoisin sauce

2 tablespoons cornstarch

1 to 2 teaspoons Chinese five-spice powder or curry powder*

1 cup frozen peas

Hot cooked rice

Chopped fresh cilantro (optional)

Chinese five-spice powder consists of cinnamon, cloves, fennel seed, star anise and Szechuan peppercorns. It can be found at Asian markets and in most supermarkets.

1. Layer onions, beef, celery, carrots and mushrooms in **CROCK-POT**® slow cooker.

2. Combine orange juice, broth, hoisin sauce, cornstarch and five-spice powder in small bowl; stir to blend. Pour into **CROCK-POT**® slow cooker. Cover; cook on HIGH 5 hours.

3. Stir in peas. Cover; cook on HIGH 20 minutes or until peas are tender. Serve over rice. Garnish with cilantro.

PORK

PORK LOIN WITH SHERRY AND RED ONIONS

Makes 8 servings

2½ pounds boneless pork loin, tied

½ teaspoon salt

½ teaspoon black pepper

2 tablespoons unsalted butter

3 large red onions, thinly sliced

1 cup pearl onions, blanched and peeled

½ cup dry sherry

2 tablespoons chopped fresh Italian parsley

2 tablespoons water

1½ tablespoons cornstarch

1. Rub pork with salt and pepper. Place pork in **CROCK-POT**® slow cooker. Melt butter in medium skillet over medium heat. Add red and pearl onions; cook and stir 5 to 7 minutes or until softened.

2. Add onion mixture, sherry and parsley to **CROCK-POT**® slow cooker over pork. Cover; cook on LOW 8 to 10 hours or on HIGH 4 to 5 hours.

3. Remove pork to large cutting board; cover loosely with foil. Let stand 10 to 15 minutes before slicing.

4. Stir water into cornstarch in small bowl until smooth; whisk into cooking liquid. Cover; cook on HIGH 15 minutes or until thickened. Serve pork with onions and sherry sauce.

TIP | Double all ingredients except for the sherry, water and cornstarch if using a 5-, 6- or 7-quart **CROCK-POT**® slow cooker.

VEGETABLE-STUFFED PORK CHOPS

Makes 4 servings

4 lean bone-in pork chops
  Salt and black pepper
1 cup frozen corn
1 medium green bell pepper,
  chopped

½ cup Italian-style seasoned
  dry bread crumbs
1 small onion, chopped
½ cup uncooked converted long
  grain rice
1 can (8 ounces) tomato sauce

1. Cut pocket into each pork chop, cutting from edge to bone. Lightly season pockets with salt and black pepper. Combine corn, bell pepper, bread crumbs, onion and rice in large bowl; stir to blend. Stuff pork chops with rice mixture. Secure open side with toothpicks.

2. Place any remaining rice mixture in **CROCK-POT**® slow cooker; top with stuffed pork chops. Pour tomato sauce over pork chops. Cover; cook on LOW 8 to 10 hours.

3. Remove pork chops to large serving platter. Remove and discard toothpicks. Serve with extra rice mixture.

TIP | Your butcher can cut a pocket in the pork chops to save you time and to ensure even cooking.

MAPLE-DRY RUBBED RIBS

Makes 4 servings

2 teaspoons chili powder, divided

1 teaspoon ground coriander

1 teaspoon garlic powder, divided

½ teaspoon salt

¼ teaspoon black pepper

3 to 3½ pounds pork baby back ribs, trimmed and cut in half

3 tablespoons maple syrup, divided

1 can (about 8 ounces) tomato sauce

¼ teaspoon ground cinnamon

¼ teaspoon ground ginger

1. Coat inside of **CROCK-POT**® slow cooker with nonstick cooking spray. Combine 1 teaspoon chili powder, coriander, ½ teaspoon garlic powder, salt and pepper in small bowl; stir to blend. Brush ribs with 1 tablespoon syrup; rub with spice mixture. Remove ribs to **CROCK-POT**® slow cooker.

2. Combine tomato sauce, remaining 1 teaspoon chili powder, ½ teaspoon garlic powder, 2 tablespoons syrup, cinnamon and ginger in medium bowl; stir to blend. Pour tomato sauce mixture over ribs in **CROCK-POT**® slow cooker. Cover; cook on LOW 8 to 9 hours.

3. Remove ribs to large serving platter; cover with foil to keep warm. Turn **CROCK-POT**® slow cooker to HIGH. Cover; cook on HIGH 10 to 15 minutes or until sauce is thickened. Brush ribs with sauce and serve any remaining sauce on the side.

SOUTHERN SMOTHERED PORK CHOPS

Makes 6 to 8 servings

6 to 8 bone-in pork chops
Salt and black pepper

2 tablespoons vegetable oil

3 cups water

1 can (10½ ounces) cream of mushroom soup

1 large onion, chopped

5 cloves garlic, chopped

2 tablespoons Italian seasoning

1 package (about ½ ounce) pork gravy mix

1 package (about 1 ounce) mushroom and onion soup mix

Corn on the cob (optional)

1. Season pork with salt and pepper. Heat oil in large skillet over medium-high heat. Add pork; brown 3 to 4 minutes on each side.

2. Place pork, water, soup, onion, garlic, Italian seasoning, gravy mix and dry soup mix in **CROCK-POT®** slow cooker. Cover; cook on LOW 5 hours. Serve with corn, if desired.

PULLED PORK WITH HONEY-CHIPOTLE BARBECUE SAUCE

Makes 8 servings

3 teaspoons chili powder, divided

1 teaspoon chipotle chili powder, divided

1 teaspoon ground cumin, divided

1 teaspoon garlic powder, divided

1 teaspoon salt

1 bone-in pork shoulder (3½ pounds), trimmed

1 can (15 ounces) tomato sauce

5 tablespoons honey, divided

1. Coat inside of **CROCK-POT**® slow cooker with nonstick cooking spray. Combine 1 teaspoon chili powder, ½ teaspoon chipotle chili powder, ½ teaspoon cumin, ½ teaspoon garlic powder and salt in small bowl. Rub pork with chili powder mixture. Place pork in **CROCK-POT**® slow cooker.

2. Combine tomato sauce, 4 tablespoons honey, remaining 2 teaspoons chili powder, ½ teaspoon chipotle chili powder, ½ teaspoon cumin and ½ teaspoon garlic powder in large bowl; stir to blend. Pour tomato mixture over pork in **CROCK-POT**® slow cooker. Cover; cook on LOW 8 hours.

3. Remove pork to large bowl; cover loosely with foil. Turn **CROCK-POT**® slow cooker to HIGH. Cover; cook on HIGH 30 minutes or until sauce is thickened. Stir in remaining 1 tablespoon honey. Turn off heat.

4. Remove pork to large cutting board. Remove bone; discard. Shred pork using two forks. Stir shredded pork back into **CROCK-POT**® slow cooker.

PINEAPPLE AND PORK TERIYAKI

Makes 6 to 8 servings

Nonstick cooking spray

2 pork tenderloins (1¼ pounds *each*)

1 can (8 ounces) pineapple chunks

½ cup teriyaki sauce

3 tablespoons honey

1 tablespoon minced fresh ginger

1. Spray large skillet with cooking spray; heat over medium-high heat. Add pork; cook 6 to 8 minutes or until browned on all sides. Remove to **CROCK-POT**® slow cooker.

2. Combine pineapple, teriyaki sauce, honey and ginger in large bowl; stir to blend. Pour over pork. Cover; cook on LOW 6 to 7 hours or on HIGH 3 to 4 hours. Remove pork to large cutting board; cover loosely with foil. Let stand 15 minutes before slicing.

3. Cover; cook on HIGH 10 to 15 minutes or until sauce is thickened. Serve sliced pork with pineapple and cooking liquid.

SAVORY SLOW COOKER PORK ROAST

Makes 8 servings

1 boneless pork blade or sirloin
  roast (3 to 4 pounds)
  Salt and black pepper
2 tablespoons vegetable oil
1 medium onion, sliced into
  ¼-inch-thick rings

2 to 3 cloves garlic, chopped
1 can (15 ounces) chicken broth
  Chopped fresh oregano
  (optional)

1. Season pork with salt and pepper. Heat oil in large skillet over medium heat; cook roast 6 to 8 minutes or until browned on all sides.

2. Place onion slices on bottom of **CROCK-POT**® slow cooker; sprinkle with garlic. Place roast on onions; pour broth over roast.

3. Cover; cook on LOW 10 hours or on HIGH 6 to 7 hours. Garnish with oregano.

CUBAN PORK SANDWICHES

Makes 8 servings

1 pork loin roast (about 2 pounds)
½ cup orange juice
2 tablespoons lime juice
1 tablespoon minced garlic
1½ teaspoons salt
½ teaspoon red pepper flakes
2 tablespoons yellow mustard

8 crusty bread rolls, split in half (6 inches *each*)
8 slices Swiss cheese
8 thin ham slices
4 small dill pickles, thinly sliced lengthwise
Nonstick cooking spray

1. Coat inside of **CROCK-POT**® slow cooker with nonstick cooking spray. Add pork.

2. Combine orange juice, lime juice, garlic, salt and red pepper flakes in small bowl; stir to blend. Pour over pork. Cover; cook on LOW 7 to 8 hours or on HIGH 3½ to 4 hours. Remove pork to large cutting board. Cover loosely with foil; let stand 10 to 15 minutes before slicing.

3. To serve, spread mustard on both sides of rolls. Divide pork slices among roll bottoms. Top with Swiss cheese slice, ham slice and pickle slices; top with roll top.

4. If desired, coat large skillet with cooking spray; heat over medium heat. Working in batches, arrange sandwiches in skillet. Cover with foil and top with dinner plate to press down sandwiches. (If necessary, weigh down with 2 to 3 cans to compress sandwiches lightly.) Heat 8 minutes or until cheese is slightly melted.*

Or use tabletop grill to compress and heat sandwiches.

SWEET AND SPICY PORK PICADILLO

Makes 4 servings

1 tablespoon olive oil

1 yellow onion, cut into ¼-inch pieces

2 cloves garlic, minced

1 pound boneless pork country-style ribs, trimmed and cut into 1-inch cubes

1 can (about 14 ounces) diced tomatoes

3 tablespoons cider vinegar

2 canned chipotle peppers in adobo sauce, chopped*

½ cup raisins

½ teaspoon ground cumin

½ teaspoon ground cinnamon

Hot cooked rice (optional)

Black beans (optional)

*You may substitute dried chipotle peppers, soaked in warm water about 20 minutes to soften before chopping.

1. Heat oil in large skillet over medium-low heat. Add onion and garlic; cook and stir 4 minutes. Add pork; cook and stir 6 to 8 minutes or until browned. Remove to **CROCK-POT**® slow cooker.

2. Combine tomatoes, vinegar, chipotle peppers, raisins, cumin and cinnamon in medium bowl; stir to blend. Pour over pork in **CROCK-POT**® slow cooker. Cover; cook on LOW 5 hours or on HIGH 3 hours. Remove pork to large cutting board; shred with two forks. Serve with rice and beans, if desired.

ANDOUILLE AND CABBAGE

Makes 8 servings

Nonstick cooking spray

1 pound andouille sausage, cut evenly into 3- to 4-inch pieces

1 small head cabbage, cut evenly into 8 wedges

1 medium onion, cut into ½-inch wedges

3 medium carrots, quartered lengthwise and cut into 3-inch pieces

8 new potatoes, cut in half

½ cup apple juice

1 can (about 14 ounces) chicken broth

1. Coat inside of **CROCK-POT**® slow cooker with cooking spray. Spray large skillet with cooking spray; heat over medium-high heat. Add sausage; cook and stir 6 to 8 minutes or until browned. Remove from heat.

2. Add cabbage, onion, carrots, potatoes, apple juice and broth to **CROCK-POT**® slow cooker; top with sausage. Cover; cook on HIGH 4 hours. Remove with slotted spoon to large serving bowl.

TIP | Andouille is a spicy, smoked pork sausage. Feel free to substitute your favorite smoked sausage or kielbasa.

SIMPLE SHREDDED PORK TACOS

Makes 6 servings

1 boneless pork shoulder roast (2 pounds)

1 cup salsa

1 can (4 ounces) chopped mild green chiles

½ teaspoon garlic salt

½ teaspoon black pepper

Flour or corn tortillas

Optional toppings: salsa, sour cream, diced tomatoes, shredded cheese and/or shredded lettuce

1. Place roast, 1 cup salsa, chiles, garlic salt and pepper in **CROCK-POT**® slow cooker. Cover; cook on LOW 8 hours or until meat is tender.

2. Remove pork to large cutting board; shred with two forks. Serve on tortillas with sauce and desired toppings.

PORK IN CHILE SAUCE

Makes 4 servings

- 2 cups tomato purée
- 2 large tomatoes, chopped
- 2 small poblano peppers, seeded and chopped
- 2 large shallots *or* 1 small onion, chopped
- 2 cloves garlic, minced
- ½ teaspoon dried oregano
- ¼ teaspoon chipotle chili powder*

- ¼ teaspoon black pepper
- 2 boneless pork chops (6 ounces *each*), cut into 1-inch pieces
- ½ teaspoon salt
- 4 whole wheat or corn tortillas, warmed

Chipotle chili powder is available in the spice section of most supermarkets.

Combine tomato purée, tomatoes, poblano peppers, shallots, garlic, oregano, chili powder and black pepper in **CROCK-POT**® slow cooker; stir to blend. Add pork. Cover; cook on LOW 5 to 6 hours. Season with salt. Serve in tortillas.

BONELESS PORK ROAST WITH GARLIC

Makes 4 to 6 servings

1 boneless pork rib roast (2 to 2½ pounds)

Salt and black pepper

3 tablespoons olive oil, divided

4 cloves garlic, minced

¼ cup chopped fresh rosemary

½ lemon, cut into ⅛- to ¼-inch slices

½ cup chicken broth

¼ cup dry white wine

1. Season pork with salt and pepper. Combine 2 tablespoons oil, garlic and rosemary in small bowl. Rub over pork. Roll and tie pork with kitchen string. Tuck lemon slices under string and into ends of roast.

2. Heat remaining 1 tablespoon oil in skillet over medium heat. Add pork; cook 6 to 8 minutes or until browned on all sides. Remove to **CROCK-POT**® slow cooker.

3. Return skillet to heat. Add broth and wine, scraping up any browned bits from bottom of skillet. Pour over pork in **CROCK-POT**® slow cooker. Cover; cook on LOW 8 to 9 hours or on HIGH 3½ to 4 hours.

4. Remove roast to large cutting board. Cover loosely with foil; let stand 10 to 15 minutes before removing kitchen string and slicing. Pour pan juices over sliced pork to serve.

SAUCY PORK LOIN AND POTATOES

Makes 6 servings

1 tablespoon olive oil

1 pork tenderloin (2 pounds)

½ cup chicken broth

3 tablespoons cornstarch

½ cup packed brown sugar

⅓ cup soy sauce

¼ cup lemon juice

¼ cup dry white wine

2 cloves garlic, minced

1 tablespoon mustard

1 tablespoon Worcestershire sauce

3 cups unpeeled potatoes, cut into wedges

Chopped fresh Italian parsley (optional)

1. Heat oil in large skillet over medium-high heat. Add pork; cook 6 to 8 minutes on each side until browned. Stir broth into cornstarch in small bowl until smooth. Place pork, broth mixture, brown sugar, soy sauce, lemon juice, wine, garlic, mustard and Worcestershire sauce in **CROCK-POT**® slow cooker. Cover; cook on LOW 4 hours.

2. Stir potatoes into **CROCK-POT**® slow cooker; turn tenderloin. Cover; cook on LOW 2 hours. Garnish with parsley.

BEEF AND LAMB

BRAISED LAMB SHANKS

Makes 4 servings

4 (12- to 16-ounce) lamb shanks

¾ teaspoon salt, divided

¼ teaspoon black pepper

1 tablespoon olive oil

1 medium onion, chopped

2 stalks celery, chopped

2 carrots, chopped

6 cloves garlic, minced

1 teaspoon dried basil

1 can (about 14 ounces) diced tomatoes

2 tablespoons tomato paste

Chopped fresh Italian parsley (optional)

1. Coat inside of **CROCK-POT**® slow cooker with nonstick cooking spray. Season lamb with ½ teaspoon salt and pepper. Heat oil in large skillet over medium-high heat. Add lamb; cook 8 to 10 minutes or until browned on all sides. Remove lamb to **CROCK-POT**® slow cooker.

2. Return skillet to medium-high heat. Add onion, celery, carrots, garlic and basil; cook and stir 3 to 4 minutes or until vegetables are softened. Add tomatoes, tomato paste and remaining ¼ teaspoon salt; cook and stir 2 to 3 minutes or until slightly thickened. Pour tomato mixture over lamb shanks in **CROCK-POT**® slow cooker.

3. Cover; cook on LOW 8 to 9 hours or until lamb is very tender. Remove lamb to large serving platter; cover to keep warm. Turn **CROCK-POT**® slow cooker to HIGH. Cook, uncovered, on HIGH 10 to 15 minutes or until sauce is thickened. Serve lamb with sauce. Garnish with parsley.

SAUVIGNON BLANC BEEF WITH BEETS AND THYME

Makes 6 servings

1 pound red or yellow beets, quartered

1 tablespoon extra virgin olive oil

3 pounds boneless beef chuck roast*

1 medium yellow onion, quartered

2 cloves garlic, minced

5 sprigs fresh thyme

1 whole bay leaf

2 whole cloves

1 cup chicken broth

1 cup Sauvignon Blanc or other dry white wine

2 tablespoons tomato paste

Salt and black pepper

*Unless you have a 5-, 6- or 7-quart CROCK-POT® slow cooker, cut any roast larger than 2½ pounds in half so it cooks completely.

1. Layer beets evenly in **CROCK-POT®** slow cooker.

2. Heat oil in large skillet over medium heat. Add roast; cook 5 to 7 minutes or until browned on all sides. Add onion and garlic during last few minutes of browning. Remove to **CROCK-POT®** slow cooker. Add thyme, bay leaf and cloves.

3. Combine broth, wine and tomato paste in medium bowl; stir until blended. Season with salt and pepper. Pour over roast and beets. Cover; cook on LOW 8 to 10 hours. Remove and discard bay leaf.

AUTUMN APRICOT BEEF RAGOÛT

Makes 3 to 4 servings

1 pound boneless beef round steak, cut into 1-inch pieces

⅔ cup apricot nectar

1 cup medium chunky salsa

1 teaspoon pumpkin pie spice

¼ teaspoon salt

½ cup chopped dried apricots

½ cup sliced green onions

3 tablespoons water

2 tablespoons all-purpose flour

3 cups hot cooked rice

¼ cup chopped fresh cilantro

1. Place beef, nectar, salsa, pumpkin pie spice and salt in **CROCK-POT**® slow cooker. Cover; cook on LOW 8 to 10 hours.

2. Turn **CROCK-POT**® slow cooker to HIGH. Add apricots and green onions. Cover; cook on HIGH 10 minutes.

3. Stir water into flour in small bowl until smooth; whisk into **CROCK-POT**® slow cooker. Cover; cook on HIGH 15 minutes or until thickened.

4. Serve over rice. Garnish with cilantro.

SHREDDED BEEF FAJITAS

Makes 12 servings

- 1 beef flank steak (about 1½ pounds), cut into 6 pieces
- 1 can (about 14 ounces) diced tomatoes with mild green chiles
- 1 cup chopped onion
- 1 medium green bell pepper, chopped
- 2 cloves garlic, minced
- 1 package (about 1½ ounces) fajita seasoning mix
- 12 (8-inch) flour tortillas
  Optional toppings: chopped fresh cilantro, guacamole, shredded Cheddar cheese and/or salsa

1. Place beef in **CROCK-POT**® slow cooker. Combine tomatoes, onion, bell pepper, garlic and fajita seasoning mix in medium bowl; pour over steak. Cover; cook on LOW 8 to 10 hours or on HIGH 4 to 5 hours.

2. Remove beef to large cutting board; shred with two forks. Stir shredded beef back into **CROCK-POT**® slow cooker to coat with sauce. Divide beef evenly among tortillas. Top as desired.

HUNGARIAN LAMB GOULASH

Makes 6 servings

- 1 package (16 ounces) frozen cut green beans, thawed
- 1 cup chopped onion
- 1¼ pounds lamb stew meat
- 1 can (15 ounces) chunky tomato sauce
- 1½ cups chicken broth
- 1 can (6 ounces) tomato paste
- 4 teaspoons paprika
- 3 cups hot cooked egg noodles

1. Place green beans and onion in **CROCK-POT**® slow cooker; top with lamb.

2. Combine tomato sauce, broth, tomato paste and paprika in large bowl; mix well. Pour over lamb mixture. Cover; cook on LOW 6 to 8 hours. Serve over noodles.

GINGER BEEF WITH PEPPERS AND MUSHROOMS

Makes 6 servings

1½ pounds boneless beef top round steak, cut into ¾-inch cubes

24 baby carrots

1 onion, chopped

1 red bell pepper, chopped

1 green bell pepper, chopped

1 package (8 ounces) mushrooms, cut into halves

1 cup beef broth

½ cup hoisin sauce

¼ cup quick-cooking tapioca

2 tablespoons grated fresh ginger

Hot cooked rice

Combine beef, carrots, onion, bell peppers, mushrooms, broth, hoisin sauce, tapioca and ginger in **CROCK-POT**® slow cooker. Cover; cook on LOW 8 to 9 hours. Serve over rice.

TIP | Boneless beef top round steak can also sometimes be found in the meat section packaged as London Broil. Both are the same cut of beef, however, London Broil is thicker.

EASY BEEF BURGUNDY

Makes 4 to 6 servings

1½ pounds boneless beef round steak, cut into 1-inch pieces

1 can (10¾ ounces) condensed cream of mushroom soup, undiluted

1 cup dry red wine

1 onion, chopped

1 can (4 ounces) sliced mushrooms, drained

1 package (about 1 ounce) onion soup mix

1 tablespoon minced garlic

Hot cooked egg noodles (optional)

Combine beef, mushroom soup, wine, onion, mushrooms, dry soup mix and garlic in **CROCK-POT®** slow cooker. Cover; cook on LOW 6 to 8 hours or until beef is tender. Serve over noodles, if desired.

BEEFY TOSTADA PIE

Makes 4 to 6 servings

2 teaspoons olive oil

1½ cups chopped onion

2 pounds ground beef

1 teaspoon salt

1 teaspoon ground cumin

1 teaspoon chili powder

2 cloves garlic, minced

1 can (15 ounces) tomato sauce

1 cup sliced black olives

8 (6-inch) flour tortillas

3½ cups (14 ounces) shredded Cheddar cheese

Sour cream, salsa and chopped green onion (optional)

1. Heat oil in large skillet over medium heat. Add onion; cook and stir 3 to 5 minutes or until tender. Add beef, salt, cumin, chili powder and garlic; cook and stir 6 to 8 minutes or until beef is browned. Drain fat. Stir in tomato sauce; cook until heated through. Stir in olives.

2. Make foil handles using three 18×2-inch strips of heavy-duty foil or use regular foil folded to double thickness. Crisscross foil in spoke design; place across bottom and up side of **CROCK-POT**® slow cooker. Lay 1 tortilla on foil strips. Spread with meat sauce and ½ cup cheese. Top with another tortilla, meat sauce and cheese. Repeat layers five times, ending with tortilla. Cover; cook on HIGH 1½ hours.

3. Lift out of **CROCK-POT**® slow cooker using foil handles; remove to large serving platter. Discard foil. Cut into wedges. Serve with sour cream, salsa and green onion, if desired.

MEATBALLS AND SPAGHETTI SAUCE

Makes 6 to 8 servings

2 pounds ground beef
1 cup plain dry bread crumbs
1 onion, chopped
2 eggs, beaten
¼ cup minced fresh Italian parsley
4 teaspoons minced garlic, divided
½ teaspoon dry mustard

½ teaspoon black pepper
4 tablespoons olive oil, divided
1 can (28 ounces) whole tomatoes
½ cup chopped fresh basil
1 teaspoon sugar
Salt and black pepper
Hot cooked spaghetti

1. Combine beef, bread crumbs, onion, eggs, parsley, 2 teaspoons garlic, dry mustard and ½ teaspoon pepper in large bowl. Form into walnut-sized balls. Heat 2 tablespoons oil in large skillet over medium heat. Add meatballs; cook 6 to 8 minutes until browned on all sides. Remove to **CROCK-POT**® slow cooker.

2. Combine tomatoes, basil, remaining 2 tablespoons oil, remaining 2 teaspoons garlic and sugar in medium bowl. Season with salt and black pepper; stir to blend. Pour over meatballs, turn to coat. Cover; cook on LOW 3 to 5 hours or on HIGH 2 to 4 hours. Serve over spaghetti.

TIP | Recipe can be doubled for a 5-, 6- or 7-quart **CROCK-POT**® slow cooker.

PHILLY CHEESE STEAKS

Makes 8 servings

2 pounds beef round steak, sliced

4 onions, sliced

2 green bell peppers, sliced

2 tablespoons butter, melted

1 tablespoon garlic-pepper seasoning

Salt

½ cup water

2 teaspoons beef bouillon granules

8 crusty Italian or French rolls, sliced in half

8 slices Cheddar cheese, cut in half

1. Combine steak, onions, bell peppers, butter, garlic-pepper seasoning and salt in **CROCK-POT**® slow cooker.

2. Whisk together water and bouillon in small bowl; pour into **CROCK-POT**® slow cooker. Cover; cook on LOW 6 to 8 hours.

3. Remove beef, onions and bell peppers from **CROCK-POT**® slow cooker. Place beef mixture on rolls. Top with cheese. If desired, place sandwiches under broiler until cheese is melted.

LAMB SHANKS AND GARLIC EGGPLANT

Makes 4 servings

2 pounds eggplant, cut into 1-inch-thick slices	1 teaspoon salt
Nonstick cooking spray	¼ teaspoon black pepper
1 medium onion, chopped	½ cup dry red wine
12 cloves garlic, crushed	1 can (about 14 ounces) diced fire-roasted tomatoes
3 lamb shanks (1 pound *each*)	Pita bread rounds (optional)

1. Preheat broiler. Place eggplant on large baking sheet; spray with cooking spray. Broil 6 to 8 minutes or until golden brown. Turn and coat with cooking spray; broil 6 to 8 minutes or until golden brown. Remove to **CROCK-POT**® slow cooker.

2. Spray large skillet with cooking spray; heat over medium-high heat. Add onion; cook 5 to 6 minutes or until golden. Sprinkle onion and garlic over eggplant.

3. Season lamb shanks with salt and pepper. Cook in same skillet over medium-high heat 5 to 7 minutes or until browned on all sides. Remove to **CROCK-POT**® slow cooker using slotted spoon.

4. Add wine to skillet; cook and stir until reduced by half. Stir in tomatoes; pour over lamb. Cover; cook on LOW 7 to 8 hours or on HIGH 3 to 4 hours.

5. Turn off heat. Remove lamb and vegetables from **CROCK-POT**® slow cooker to large cutting board. Use fork to slide meat off bones. Let cooking liquid stand 5 minutes. Skim off and discard fat. Serve lamb and vegetables with cooking liquid. Serve with pita rounds, if desired.

CLASSIC POT ROAST

Makes 6 to 8 servings

1 tablespoon vegetable oil

1 boneless beef chuck shoulder roast (3 to 4 pounds)*

6 medium potatoes, cut into halves

6 carrots, chunks

2 medium onions, cut into quarters

2 stalks celery, sliced

1 can (about 14 ounces) diced tomatoes

Salt and black pepper

Dried oregano

2 tablespoons water

1½ to 2 tablespoons all-purpose flour

*Unless you have a 5-, 6- or 7-quart CROCK-POT® slow cooker, cut any roast larger than 2½ pounds in half so it cooks completely.

1. Heat oil in large skillet over medium-low heat. Add roast; cook 6 to 8 minutes or until browned on all sides. Remove to **CROCK-POT®** slow cooker.

2. Add potatoes, carrots, onions, celery and tomatoes. Season with salt, pepper and oregano. Add enough water to cover bottom of **CROCK-POT®** slow cooker by about ½ inch. Cover; cook on LOW 8 to 10 hours.

3. Turn off heat. Remove roast and vegetables to large serving platter using slotted spoon. Let cooking liquid stand 5 minutes. Skim off fat and discard. Turn **CROCK-POT®** slow cooker to HIGH. Stir water into flour in small bowl until smooth; whisk into cooking liquid. Cover; cook on HIGH 10 to 15 minutes or until thickened. Serve sauce over roast and vegetables.

MOROCCAN-STYLE LAMB SHOULDER CHOPS WITH COUSCOUS

Makes 4 servings

4 lamb blade chops (about 2½ pounds)

Salt and black pepper

1 tablespoon olive oil

1 onion, chopped

1 clove garlic, minced

1 teaspoon grated fresh ginger

¼ teaspoon ground cinnamon

½ teaspoon ground turmeric

½ teaspoon salt

¼ teaspoon black pepper

1 whole bay leaf

1 can (about 14 ounces) diced tomatoes, undrained

1 cup canned chickpeas, rinsed and drained

½ cup water

2 tablespoons lemon juice

Hot cooked couscous

Lemon wedges (optional)

1. Coat inside of **CROCK-POT**® slow cooker with nonstick cooking spray. Season lamb chops with salt and pepper. Heat oil in large skillet over medium-high heat. Add lamb chops; cook 5 to 7 minutes or until browned on all sides. Remove to **CROCK-POT**® slow cooker.

2. Add onion to skillet; cook and stir 2 to 3 minutes or until translucent. Add garlic, ginger, cinnamon, turmeric, ½ teaspoon salt, ¼ teaspoon pepper and bay leaf; cook and stir 30 seconds. Stir in tomatoes, chickpeas, water and lemon juice; bring to a simmer. Pour mixture over lamb. Cover; cook on HIGH 3½ to 4 hours or until lamb is tender.

3. Remove and discard bay leaf. Serve lamb chops over couscous with sauce and vegetables. Serve with lemon wedges, if desired.

TIP | Adding fresh lemon juice just before serving enhances the flavor of many dishes. Try it with other dishes prepared in your **CROCK-POT**® slow cooker.

MAPLE WHISKEY-GLAZED BEEF BRISKET

Makes 4 to 6 servings

1 teaspoon ground red pepper

1 tablespoon coarse salt

½ teaspoon black pepper

1½ to 2 pounds beef brisket, scored with a knife on both sides

2 tablespoons olive oil

½ cup maple syrup

¼ cup whiskey

2 tablespoons packed brown sugar

1 tablespoon tomato paste

Juice of 1 orange

2 cloves garlic, crushed

4 (¹⁄₁₆-inch-thick) slices fresh ginger

4 (½×1½-inch-thick) slices orange peel

1. Combine ground red pepper, salt and black pepper in small mixing bowl. Rub over brisket. Place brisket in large resealable food storage bag.

2. Combine oil, syrup, whiskey, brown sugar, tomato paste, orange juice, garlic, ginger and orange peel in small bowl; stir to blend. Pour mixture over brisket in resealable food storage bag. Marinate brisket in refrigerator, at least 2 hours or overnight.

3. Remove brisket and marinade to **CROCK-POT**® slow cooker. Cover, cook on LOW 7 to 9 hours, turning brisket once or twice. Slice thinly across the grain to serve.

BEEFY TORTELLINI

Makes 6 servings

½ pound ground beef

1 jar (24 to 26 ounces) roasted tomato and garlic pasta sauce

1 package (12 ounces) uncooked three-cheese tortellini

8 ounces sliced button or exotic mushrooms, such as oyster, shiitake and cremini

½ cup water

½ teaspoon red pepper flakes (optional)

¾ cup grated Asiago or Romano cheese

Chopped fresh Italian parsley (optional)

1. Coat inside of **CROCK-POT**® slow cooker with nonstick cooking spray. Brown beef in large skillet over medium-high heat 6 to 8 minutes, stirring to break up meat. Remove to **CROCK-POT**® slow cooker using slotted spoon.

2. Stir pasta sauce, tortellini, mushrooms, water and red pepper flakes, if desired, into **CROCK-POT**® slow cooker. Cover; cook on LOW 2 hours or on HIGH 1 hour. Stir.

3. Cover; cook on LOW 2 to 2½ hours or on HIGH ½ to 1 hour. Serve in shallow bowls topped with cheese and parsley, if desired.

WINE-BRAISED BONELESS LEG OF LAMB

Makes about 8 servings

1½ cups beef broth
¼ cup all-purpose flour
2 tablespoons tomato paste
1 teaspoon dried mint
1 teaspoon dried basil
1 teaspoon dried oregano
1 teaspoon salt, divided
½ teaspoon garlic powder
½ teaspoon black pepper, divided
24 baby new potatoes (about 1 pound)

24 baby carrots
1 ounce dried porcini mushrooms (optional)
1 tablespoon olive oil
3 to 3½ pounds boneless leg of lamb, trimmed and tied
1 large onion, thinly sliced
4 cloves garlic, thinly sliced
¾ cup dry red wine
Sprig fresh oregano (optional)

1. Coat inside of **CROCK-POT**® slow cooker with nonstick cooking spray. Combine broth, flour, tomato paste, mint, basil, dried oregano, ½ teaspoon salt, garlic powder and ¼ teaspoon pepper in medium bowl. Pour broth mixture into **CROCK-POT**® slow cooker. Add potatoes, carrots and mushrooms, if desired.

2. Heat oil in large skillet over medium-high heat. Season lamb with remaining ½ teaspoon salt and ¼ teaspoon pepper. Add to skillet; cook and turn 8 to 12 minutes or until well browned. Remove lamb to **CROCK-POT**® slow cooker on top of vegetables.

3. Return skillet to medium-high heat. Add onion and garlic; cook and stir 5 to 6 minutes or until onion is softened. Add wine. Bring to a boil; cook 2 minutes. Pour onion mixture over lamb. Cover; cook on LOW 8 to 9 hours or on HIGH 4 to 5 hours. Garnish with fresh oregano.

HORSERADISH ROAST BEEF AND POTATOES

Makes 12 servings

1 tablespoon minced fresh Italian parsley

1 teaspoon dried thyme, basil or oregano

1 tablespoon freshly grated horseradish

1 tablespoon Dijon mustard

3 pounds beef chuck roast*

1 to 2 pounds Yukon Gold potatoes, quartered

1 pound mushrooms, cut into large pieces

2 cans (about 14 ounces *each*) beef broth

2 large tomatoes, seeded and diced

1 large onion, sliced

1 green bell pepper, chopped

1 red bell pepper, chopped

1 cup dry red wine

3 cloves garlic, minced

1 whole bay leaf

Salt and black pepper

Unless you have a 5-, 6- or 7-quart CROCK-POT® slow cooker, cut any roast larger than 2½ pounds in half so it cooks completely.

1. Combine parsley, thyme, horseradish and mustard in small bowl; stir to make a paste. Place roast in **CROCK-POT®** slow cooker; spread paste over roast.

2. Add potatoes, mushrooms, broth, tomatoes, onion, bell peppers, wine, garlic and bay leaf to **CROCK-POT®** slow cooker. Season with salt and black pepper; stir to blend. Add enough water to cover roast and vegetables. Cover; cook on HIGH 2 hours. Turn **CROCK-POT®** slow cooker to LOW. Cover; cook on LOW 4 to 6 hours. Remove and discard bay leaf.

SICILIAN STEAK PINWHEELS

Makes 4 to 6 servings

¾ **pound mild or hot Italian sausage, casings removed**

1¾ **cups fresh bread crumbs**

¾ **cup grated Parmesan cheese**

2 **eggs**

3 **tablespoons minced fresh Italian parsley, plus additional for garnish**

1½ **to 2 pounds beef round steak**

1 **cup frozen peas**

1 **cup pasta sauce**

1 **cup beef broth**

1. Coat inside of **CROCK-POT**® slow cooker with nonstick cooking spray. Combine sausage, bread crumbs, cheese, eggs and 3 tablespoons parsley in large bowl; stir to blend.

2. Place round steak between two large sheets of plastic wrap. Using tenderizer mallet or back of skillet, pound steak until meat is about ⅜ inch thick. Remove top layer of plastic wrap. Spread sausage mixture over steak. Press frozen peas into sausage mixture. Lift edge of plastic wrap at short end; roll up steak completely. Tie at 2-inch intervals with kitchen string. Remove to **CROCK-POT**® slow cooker.

3. Combine pasta sauce and broth in medium bowl. Pour over steak. Cover; cook on LOW 6 hours.

4. Turn off heat. Remove steak to large serving platter. Cover loosely with foil 10 to 15 minutes before removing string and slicing. Let cooking liquid stand 5 minutes. Skim off fat and discard. Serve steak with cooking liquid.

CHICKEN AND TURKEY

BONELESS CHICKEN CACCIATORE

Makes 6 servings

Olive oil

6 boneless, skinless chicken breasts, sliced in half horizontally

4 cups tomato-basil pasta sauce

1 cup coarsely chopped yellow onion

1 cup coarsely chopped green bell pepper

1 can (6 ounces) sliced mushrooms

¼ cup dry red wine

2 teaspoons minced garlic

2 teaspoons dried oregano

2 teaspoons dried thyme

2 teaspoons salt

2 teaspoons black pepper

Hot cooked pasta

1. Heat oil in large skillet over medium heat. Add chicken; cook 6 to 8 minutes or until browned on both sides. Remove to **CROCK-POT**® slow cooker using slotted spoon.

2. Add pasta sauce, onion, bell pepper, mushrooms, wine, garlic, oregano, thyme, salt and black pepper to **CROCK-POT**® slow cooker; stir to blend. Cover; cook on LOW 5 to 7 hours or on HIGH 2 to 3 hours. Serve over pasta.

SHREDDED CHICKEN TACOS

Makes 4 servings

2 pounds boneless, skinless chicken thighs

½ cup prepared mango salsa, plus additional for serving

Shredded lettuce

8 (6-inch) yellow corn tortillas, warmed Lettuce

1. Coat inside of **CROCK-POT®** slow cooker with nonstick cooking spray. Add chicken and ½ cup salsa. Cover; cook on LOW 4 to 5 hours or on HIGH 2½ to 3 hours.

2. Remove chicken to large cutting board; shred with two forks. Stir shredded chicken back into **CROCK-POT®** slow cooker. To serve, divide chicken and lettuce evenly among tortillas. Serve with additional salsa.

CHICKEN CONGEE

Makes 6 servings

6 cups water

4 cups chicken broth

4 chicken drumsticks

1 cup uncooked white jasmine rice, rinsed and drained

1 (1-inch) piece ginger, sliced into 4 pieces

2 teaspoons kosher salt

¼ teaspoon ground white pepper

Optional toppings: soy sauce, sesame oil, thinly sliced green onions, fried shallots, fried garlic slices, salted roasted peanuts and/or pickled vegetables

1. Add water, broth, chicken, rice, ginger, salt and white pepper to **CROCK-POT®** slow cooker. Cover; cook on LOW 8 hours or on HIGH 4 hours or until rice has completely broken down and mixture is thickened.

2. Remove and discard ginger. Remove chicken to large cutting board. Discard skin and bones. Shred chicken using two forks. Stir chicken back into **CROCK-POT®** slow cooker. Ladle congee into serving bowls; top with desired toppings.

TURKEY SPINACH LASAGNA

Makes 8 servings

Nonstick cooking spray

¾ cup chopped onion

2 cloves garlic, minced

1 pound lean ground turkey

1 teaspoon Italian seasoning

¼ teaspoon black pepper

1 container (15 ounces) ricotta cheese

1 cup (4 ounces) Italian shredded cheese blend, divided

12 ounces uncooked no-boil lasagna noodles

1 package (10 ounces) frozen chopped spinach, thawed and pressed dry

1 jar (24 to 26 ounces) chunky marinara sauce

½ cup water

1. Spray large skillet with cooking spray; heat over medium heat. Add onion and garlic; cook and stir 4 minutes. Add turkey; cook and stir 6 to 8 minutes or until no longer pink, stirring to break up meat. Season with Italian seasoning and pepper; remove from heat. Set aside.

2. Combine ricotta cheese and ½ cup Italian cheese blend in small bowl; mix well.

3. Layer half of uncooked noodles, breaking in half to fit and overlap as necessary, in **CROCK-POT**® slow cooker. Spread half of meat mixture and half of spinach over noodles. Top with half of marinara sauce and ¼ cup water. Gently spread cheese mixture on top. Continue layering with remaining noodles, meat mixture, spinach, marinara sauce and ¼ cup water.

4. Cover; cook on LOW 4 hours. To serve, sprinkle top with remaining ½ cup Italian cheese blend. Cover; cook on LOW 10 to 15 minutes or until cheese is melted. Divide evenly into eight pieces.

COQ AU VIN WITH LIMA BEANS

Makes 8 to 10 servings

4 pounds chicken thighs and drumsticks

3 slices bacon, cut into pieces

4 cups chicken broth

1 cup sliced mushrooms

1 cup sliced carrots

1 cup dry red wine

½ cup pearl onions

⅓ cup whiskey

3 to 4 cloves garlic, chopped

2 tablespoons tomato paste

1½ teaspoons herbes de Provence

2 whole bay leaves

Salt and black pepper

1 tablespoon water

2 tablespoons all-purpose flour

1 cup lima beans

Chopped fresh Italian parsley (optional)

Roasted red potatoes, quartered (optional)

1. Coat inside of **CROCK-POT®** slow cooker with nonstick cooking spray. Add chicken and bacon to **CROCK-POT®** slow cooker. Cover; cook on HIGH 45 minutes, turning chicken halfway through cooking time.

2. Turn **CROCK-POT®** slow cooker to LOW. Add broth, mushrooms, carrots, wine, onions, whiskey, garlic, tomato paste, herbes de Provence and bay leaves to **CROCK-POT®** slow cooker. Season with salt and pepper. Stir water into flour in small bowl until smooth; whisk into **CROCK-POT®** slow cooker.

3. Cover; cook on LOW 6 hours. Add beans to **CROCK-POT®** slow cooker during last 10 minutes of cooking. Remove and discard bay leaves. Garnish with parsley. Serve with potatoes, if desired.

BARBECUE TURKEY LEGS

Makes 6 servings

Barbecue Sauce
(recipe follows)

6 turkey drumsticks

2 teaspoons salt

2 teaspoons black pepper

1. Prepare Barbecue Sauce.

2. Season drumsticks with salt and pepper. Place in **CROCK-POT**® slow cooker. Add Barbecue Sauce; turn to coat. Cover; cook on LOW 7 to 8 hours or on HIGH 3 to 4 hours.

BARBECUE SAUCE

Makes about 2 cups

½ cup white vinegar

½ cup ketchup

½ cup molasses

¼ cup Worcestershire sauce

1 tablespoon onion powder

1 tablespoon garlic powder

1 teaspoon hickory liquid smoke

⅛ teaspoon chipotle chili powder

Combine vinegar, ketchup, molasses, Worcestershire sauce, onion powder, garlic powder, liquid smoke and chili powder in medium bowl; mix well.

CHICKEN PARMESAN WITH EGGPLANT

Makes 6 to 8 servings

- 6 boneless, skinless chicken breasts
- 2 eggs
- 2 teaspoons salt
- 2 teaspoons black pepper
- 2 cups seasoned dry bread crumbs
- ½ cup olive oil
- ½ cup (1 stick) butter
- 2 small eggplants, cut into ¾-inch-thick slices
- 1½ cups grated Parmesan cheese
- 2¼ cups tomato-basil pasta sauce
- 1 pound sliced or shredded mozzarella cheese

1. Slice chicken breasts in half lengthwise. Cut each half lengthwise again to get four ¾-inch slices.

2. Combine eggs, salt and pepper in medium bowl; whisk to blend. Place bread crumbs in separate medium bowl. Dip chicken in egg mixture; turn to coat. Then coat chicken with bread crumbs, covering both sides evenly.

3. Heat oil and butter in large skillet over medium heat. Add breaded chicken; cook 6 to 8 minutes or until browned on both sides. Remove to paper towel-lined plate to drain excess oil.

4. Layer half of eggplant, ¾ cup Parmesan cheese and 1 cup pasta sauce in bottom of **CROCK-POT**® slow cooker. Top with half of chicken, remaining half of eggplant, remaining ¾ cup Parmesan cheese and ¼ cup sauce. Arrange remaining half of chicken on sauce; top with remaining 1 cup sauce and mozzarella cheese. Cover; cook on LOW 6 hours or on HIGH 2 to 4 hours.

CHICKEN AND BISCUITS

Makes 4 servings

4 boneless, skinless chicken breasts, cut into 1-inch pieces

1 can (10¾ ounces) condensed cream of chicken soup

1 package (10 ounces) frozen peas and carrots

1 package (7½ ounces) refrigerated biscuits

1. Place chicken in **CROCK-POT**® slow cooker; pour in soup. Cover; cook on LOW 4 hours.

2. Stir in peas and carrots. Cover; cook on LOW 30 minutes or until vegetables are heated through.

3. Meanwhile, bake biscuits according to package directions. Spoon chicken and vegetable mixture over biscuits to serve.

LEMON AND HERB TURKEY BREAST

Makes 4 servings

- 1 split turkey breast (about 3 pounds)
- ½ cup lemon juice
- ½ cup dry white wine
- 6 cloves garlic, minced
- ¼ teaspoon salt
- ¼ teaspoon dried parsley flakes
- ¼ teaspoon dried tarragon
- ¼ teaspoon dried rosemary
- ¼ teaspoon dried sage
- ¼ teaspoon black pepper

  Sprigs fresh sage and rosemary (optional)

  Lemon slices (optional)

1. Place turkey in **CROCK-POT®** slow cooker. Combine lemon juice, wine, garlic, salt, parsley flakes, tarragon, dried rosemary, dried sage and pepper in medium bowl; stir to blend. Pour lemon juice mixture over turkey in **CROCK-POT®** slow cooker.

2. Cover; cook on LOW 8 to 10 hours or on HIGH 4 to 5 hours. Garnish with fresh sage, fresh rosemary and lemon slices.

CHICKEN VESUVIO

Makes 4 to 6 servings

3 tablespoons all-purpose flour

1½ teaspoons dried oregano

1 teaspoon salt

½ teaspoon black pepper

1 frying chicken, cut up and trimmed *or* 3 pounds bone-in chicken pieces, trimmed

2 tablespoons olive oil

4 small baking potatoes, unpeeled and cut into 8 wedges *each*

2 small onions, cut into thin wedges

4 cloves garlic, minced

¼ cup chicken broth

¼ cup dry white wine

¼ cup chopped fresh Italian parsley

Lemon wedges (optional)

1. Combine flour, oregano, salt and pepper in large resealable food storage bag. Add chicken, several pieces at a time, to bag; shake to coat lightly with flour mixture. Heat oil in large skillet over medium heat. Add chicken; cook 10 to 12 minutes or until browned on all sides.

2. Place potatoes, onions and garlic in **CROCK-POT**® slow cooker. Add broth and wine; top with chicken pieces. Pour pan juices from skillet over chicken. Cover; cook on LOW 6 to 7 hours or on HIGH 3 to 3½ hours.

3. Remove chicken and vegetables to serving plates; top with juices from **CROCK-POT**® slow cooker. Sprinkle with parsley. Serve with lemon wedges, if desired.

CHICKEN AND SPICY BLACK BEAN TACOS

Makes 6 servings

1 can (about 15 ounces) black beans, rinsed and drained

1 can (10 ounces) diced tomatoes with mild green chiles, drained

1½ teaspoons chili powder

¾ teaspoon ground cumin

1 tablespoon plus 1 teaspoon extra virgin olive oil, divided

12 ounces boneless, skinless chicken breasts

12 crisp corn taco shells

Optional toppings: shredded lettuce, diced tomatoes, shredded Cheddar cheese, sour cream and/or sliced black olives

1. Coat inside of **CROCK-POT**® slow cooker with nonstick cooking spray. Add beans and tomatoes with chiles. Combine chili powder, cumin and 1 teaspoon oil in small bowl; rub onto chicken. Place chicken in **CROCK-POT**® slow cooker. Cover; cook on HIGH 1¾ hours.

2. Remove chicken to large cutting board; slice. Remove bean mixture to large bowl using slotted spoon. Stir in remaining 1 tablespoon oil.

3. To serve, warm taco shells according to package directions. Fill with equal amounts of bean mixture and chicken. Top as desired.

BISTRO CHICKEN IN RICH CREAM SAUCE

Makes 4 servings

4 skinless, bone-in chicken breast halves, rinsed and patted dry (about 3 pounds *total*)

½ cup dry white wine, divided

1 tablespoon *or* ½ packet (about 1 ounce) Italian salad dressing and seasoning mix

½ teaspoon dried oregano

1 can (10¾ ounces) condensed cream of chicken soup, undiluted

3 ounces cream cheese, cut into cubes

¼ teaspoon salt

⅛ teaspoon black pepper

2 tablespoons chopped fresh Italian parsley (optional)

1. Coat inside of **CROCK-POT**® slow cooker with nonstick cooking spray. Arrange chicken in single layer in bottom, overlapping slightly. Pour ¼ cup wine over chicken. Sprinkle evenly with salad dressing mix and oregano. Cover; cook on LOW 5 to 6 hours or on HIGH 3 hours.

2. Remove chicken to plate with slotted spoon. Whisk soup, cream cheese, salt and pepper into cooking liquid. (Mixture will be a bit lumpy.) Arrange chicken on top. Cover; cook on HIGH 15 to 20 minutes or until heated through.

3. Remove chicken to shallow pasta bowl. Add remaining ¼ cup wine to sauce; whisk until smooth. To serve, spoon sauce around chicken; garnish with parsley.

CHICKEN AND WILD RICE CASSEROLE

Makes 4 to 6 servings

3 tablespoons olive oil

2 slices bacon, chopped

1½ pounds chicken thighs, trimmed

3 cups hot chicken broth**

6 ounces brown mushrooms, wiped clean and quartered*

1 cup uncooked converted long grain white rice

1 package (4 ounces) wild rice

½ cup diced onion

½ cup diced celery

2 tablespoons Worcestershire sauce

½ teaspoon salt

½ teaspoon dried sage

¼ teaspoon black pepper

2 tablespoons chopped fresh Italian parsley (optional)

*Use "baby bellas" or cremini mushrooms. Or you may substitute white button mushrooms.

**Use enough broth to cover chicken.

1. Spread oil on bottom of **CROCK-POT**® slow cooker. Microwave bacon on HIGH 1 minute. Remove to **CROCK-POT**® slow cooker. Place chicken in **CROCK-POT**® slow cooker, skin side down.

2. Add broth, mushrooms, white rice, wild rice, onion, celery, Worcestershire sauce, salt, sage and pepper to **CROCK-POT**® slow cooker. Cover; cook on LOW 3 to 4 hours or until rice is tender.

3. Turn off heat. Uncover; let stand 15 minutes before serving. Remove chicken skin, if desired. Garnish with chopped parsley.

HAM AND SAGE STUFFED CORNISH HENS

Makes 4 servings

1 cup plus 3 tablespoons sliced celery, divided

1 cup sliced leek (white part only)

2 tablespoons butter, divided

¼ cup finely diced onion

¼ cup diced smoked ham or prosciutto

1 cup seasoned stuffing mix

1 cup chicken broth

1 tablespoon finely chopped fresh sage *or* 1 teaspoon ground sage

4 Cornish hens (about 1½ pounds *each*)

Salt and black pepper

1. Coat inside of **CROCK-POT**® slow cooker with nonstick cooking spray. Toss 1 cup celery and leek in **CROCK-POT**® slow cooker.

2. Melt 1 tablespoon butter in large nonstick skillet over medium heat. Add remaining 3 tablespoons celery, onion and ham; cook and stir 5 minutes or until onion is softened. Stir in stuffing mix, broth and sage. Remove mixture to medium bowl.

3. Rinse hens and pat dry. Sprinkle inside and outside of each hen with salt and pepper. Gently spoon stuffing into cavities. Tie each hen's drumsticks together with kitchen string.

4. Melt remaining 1 tablespoon butter in same skillet over medium-high heat. Place 2 hens, breast sides down, in skillet; cook until skins brown, turning to brown all sides. Remove to **CROCK-POT**® slow cooker. Repeat with remaining hens.

5. Cover; cook on LOW 5 to 6 hours or on HIGH 3 to 4 hours. Remove string; place hens on serving platter. Spoon cooking broth over hens.

CHICKEN CORDON BLEU

Makes 4 servings

¼ cup all-purpose flour

1 teaspoon paprika

½ teaspoon salt

¼ teaspoon black pepper

4 boneless chicken breasts, lightly pounded*

4 slices ham

4 slices Swiss cheese

2 tablespoons olive oil

½ cup dry white wine

½ cup chicken broth

½ cup half-and-half

2 tablespoons cornstarch

Place chicken between two pieces of plastic wrap and flatten with meat mallet or back of skillet.

1. Combine flour, paprika, salt and pepper in large resealable food storage bag Place flattened chicken on large cutting board, skin side down. Place 1 slice ham and 1 slice cheese on each piece. Fold chicken up to enclose filling; secure with toothpick. Place in bag with seasoned flour; shake gently to coat.

2. Heat oil in large skillet over medium-high heat. Add chicken; cook 5 to 7 minutes or until browned on all sides. Remove to **CROCK-POT**® slow cooker.

3. Remove skillet from heat; add wine, stirring to scrape up any browned bits from bottom. Pour into **CROCK-POT**® slow cooker. Add broth. Cover; cook on LOW 2 hours.

4. Remove chicken to large serving platter using slotted spoon. Cover and keep warm. Stir half-and-half into cornstarch in small bowl until smooth; whisk into cooking liquid. Cover; cook on LOW 15 minutes or until thickened. Remove and discard toothpicks. Serve chicken with cooking liquid.

CHIPOTLE CHICKEN CASSEROLE

Makes 6 servings

1 pound boneless, skinless chicken thighs, cut into cubes

1½ cups chicken broth

1 can (about 15 ounces) navy beans, rinsed and drained

1 can (about 15 ounces) black beans, rinsed and drained

1 can (about 14 ounces) crushed tomatoes, undrained

½ cup orange juice

1 medium onion, diced

1 canned chipotle pepper in adobo sauce, minced

1 teaspoon salt

1 teaspoon ground cumin

1 whole bay leaf

Combine chicken, broth, beans, tomatoes, orange juice, onion, chipotle pepper, salt, cumin and bay leaf in **CROCK-POT®** slow cooker; stir to blend. Cover; cook on LOW 7 to 8 hours or on HIGH 3½ to 4 hours. Remove and discard bay leaf before serving.

FISH AND SEAFOOD

SEAFOOD CIOPPINO

Makes 4 servings

- 1 tablespoon olive oil
- 1 medium fennel bulb, thinly sliced
- 1 medium onion, chopped
- 4 cloves garlic, minced
- 1 teaspoon dried basil
- ¼ teaspoon saffron threads, crushed (optional)
- 1 can (about 14 ounces) diced tomatoes

- 1 bottle (8 ounces) clam juice
- 16 little neck clams, scrubbed
- 24 mussels, scrubbed
- 1 pound cod fillet, cut into 8 pieces
- 8 ounces large raw shrimp, peeled and deveined (with tails on)
- ½ teaspoon salt
- ⅛ teaspoon black pepper

1. Coat inside of **CROCK-POT**® slow cooker with nonstick cooking spray. Heat oil in large skillet over medium-high heat. Add fennel, onion, garlic, basil and saffron, if desired; cook and stir 4 to 5 minutes or until vegetables are softened. Remove onion mixture to **CROCK-POT**® slow cooker. Stir in tomatoes and clam juice.

2. Cover; cook on HIGH 2 to 3 hours. Add clams. Cover; cook on HIGH 30 minutes. Add mussels. Cover; cook on HIGH 15 minutes.

3. Season cod and shrimp with salt and pepper. Place on top of shellfish. Cover; cook on HIGH 25 to 30 minutes or until clams and mussels have opened and fish is cooked through. Discard any unopened clams or mussels.

CHEESY SHRIMP ON GRITS

Makes 6 servings

1 cup finely chopped green bell pepper

1 cup finely chopped red bell pepper

½ cup thinly sliced celery

1 bunch green onions, chopped and divided

¼ cup (½ stick) butter, cubed

1¼ teaspoons seafood seasoning

2 whole bay leaves

¼ teaspoon ground red pepper

1 pound medium raw shrimp, peeled and deveined

5⅓ cups water

1⅓ cups quick-cooking grits or polenta

2 cups (8 ounces) shredded sharp Cheddar cheese

¼ cup whipping cream or half-and-half

1. Coat inside of **CROCK-POT**® slow cooker with nonstick cooking spray. Add bell peppers, celery, all but ½ cup green onions, butter, seafood seasoning, bay leaves and ground red pepper. Cover; cook on LOW 4 hours or on HIGH 2 hours.

2. Add shrimp. Cover; cook on HIGH 15 minutes.

3. Meanwhile, bring water to a boil in medium saucepan. Add grits; cook according to package directions.

4. Remove and discard bay leaves. Stir cheese, cream and remaining ½ cup green onions into **CROCK-POT**® slow cooker. Cook, uncovered, on HIGH 5 minutes or until cheese is melted. Serve over grits.

TIP | Seafood is delicate and should be added to the **CROCK-POT**® slow cooker during the last 15 to 30 minutes of the cooking time on HIGH, and during the last 30 to 45 minutes if you're cooking on LOW. It can overcook easily, becoming tough and rubbery.

SOUTHWESTERN SALMON PO' BOYS

Makes 4 servings

1 red bell pepper, sliced

1 green bell pepper, sliced

1 onion, sliced

½ teaspoon Southwest chipotle seasoning

¼ teaspoon salt

¼ teaspoon black pepper

4 salmon fillets (about 6 ounces *each*), rinsed and patted dry

½ cup Italian dressing

¼ cup water

4 large French sandwich rolls, split and toasted

Chipotle mayonnaise*

Fresh cilantro (optional)

If unavailable, combine ¼ cup mayonnaise with ½ teaspoon adobo sauce or substitute regular mayonnaise.

1. Coat inside of **CROCK-POT**® slow cooker with nonstick cooking spray. Arrange half of sliced bell peppers and onion in bottom.

2. Combine chipotle seasoning, salt and black pepper in small bowl; rub over both sides of salmon. Place salmon on top of vegetables in **CROCK-POT**® slow cooker. Pour Italian dressing over salmon and top with remaining bell peppers and onion. Add water. Cover; cook on HIGH 1½ hours.

3. Spread tops of rolls with chipotle mayonnaise. Garnish with cilantro. Spoon 1 to 2 tablespoons cooking liquid onto roll bottoms. Place 1 salmon fillet on each roll (remove skin first, if desired). Top with vegetable mixture.

ASIAN LETTUCE WRAPS

Makes 6 servings

2 teaspoons canola oil

1½ pounds boneless, skinless chicken breasts, chopped into ¼-inch pieces

2 leeks, trimmed and chopped into ¼-inch pieces

1 cup shiitake mushrooms, stems removed and caps chopped into ¼-inch pieces

1 stalk celery, chopped into ¼-inch pieces

2 tablespoons water

1 tablespoon oyster sauce

1 tablespoon soy sauce

1 teaspoon dark sesame oil

¼ teaspoon black pepper

1 bag (8 ounces) cole slaw or broccoli slaw mix

½ red bell pepper, cut into thin strips

½ pound large raw shrimp, peeled, deveined and cut into ¼-inch pieces

3 tablespoons unsalted dry roasted peanuts, coarsely chopped

Hoisin sauce

12 crisp romaine lettuce leaves, white rib removed and patted dry

Fresh whole chives

1. Heat canola oil in large skillet over medium-high heat. Add chicken; cook 6 to 8 minutes or until browned on all sides. Remove to **CROCK-POT**® slow cooker using slotted spoon. Add leeks, mushrooms, celery, water, oyster sauce, soy sauce, sesame oil and black pepper to **CROCK-POT**® slow cooker. Toss slaw and bell pepper in medium bowl; place in single layer on top of chicken.

2. Cover; cook on LOW 4 to 5 hours or on HIGH 2 to 2½ hours or until chicken is cooked through. Stir in shrimp during last 20 minutes of cooking. When shrimp are pink and opaque, remove mixture to large bowl. Add chopped peanuts; mix well.

3. To serve, spread about 1 teaspoon hoisin sauce on each lettuce leaf. Add 1 to 2 tablespoons meat mixture and tightly roll; secure by tying chives around rolled leaves.

SHRIMP JAMBALAYA

Makes 8 servings

1 (8-ounce) box New Orleans style jambalaya mix

2½ cups water

1 can (about 14 ounces) diced tomatoes with green pepper, celery and onion

8 ounces andouille sausage, cut into ¼-inch-thick slices

1 teaspoon hot pepper sauce, plus additional for serving

1½ pounds large raw shrimp, peeled and deveined (with tails on)

1. Coat inside of **CROCK-POT®** slow cooker with nonstick cooking spray. Add jambalaya mix, water, tomatoes, sausage and 1 teaspoon hot pepper sauce; stir to blend. Cover; cook on LOW 2½ to 3 hours or until rice is cooked through.

2. Stir in shrimp. Cover; cook on LOW 30 minutes or until shrimp are pink and opaque. Serve with additional hot pepper sauce.

SALMON AND BOK CHOY

Makes 8 servings

1 cup vegetable broth

3 small heads bok choy, stems and leaves sliced

2 cloves garlic, finely chopped

2 teaspoons ground ginger

¼ teaspoon red pepper flakes

3 pounds salmon fillets

¼ cup soy sauce

¼ cup packed brown sugar

2 tablespoons lemon juice

½ teaspoon Chinese five-spice powder

4 cups cooked brown rice

1. Combine broth, bok choy stems, garlic, ginger and red pepper flakes in **CROCK-POT**® slow cooker; stir to blend. Cover; cook on LOW 4 to 6 hours or on HIGH 1½ hours or until fork-tender.

2. Stir bok choy leaves into **CROCK-POT**® slow cooker; top with salmon. Cover; cook on LOW 30 minutes or until fish is cooked through.

3. Meanwhile, whisk soy sauce, brown sugar, lemon juice and five-spice powder in small saucepan; bring to a boil. Reduce heat; simmer until reduced to ⅓ cup. Serve salmon and bok choy on rice with sauce.

BRAISED SEA BASS WITH AROMATIC VEGETABLES

Makes 6 servings

2 tablespoons butter or olive oil

2 fennel bulbs, thinly sliced

3 large carrots, julienned

3 large leeks, cleaned and thinly sliced

Salt and black pepper

6 sea bass fillets or other firm-fleshed white fish (2 to 3 pounds *total*)

1. Melt butter in large skillet over medium-high heat. Add fennel, carrots and leeks; cook and stir 6 to 8 minutes or until beginning to soften and lightly brown. Season with salt and pepper. Arrange half of vegetables in bottom of **CROCK-POT**® slow cooker.

2. Season bass with salt and pepper; place on top of vegetables in **CROCK-POT**® slow cooker. Top with remaining vegetables. Cover; cook on LOW 2 to 3 hours or on HIGH 1 to 1½ hours.

TUNA CASSEROLE

Makes 6 servings

2 cans (10¾ ounces *each*) cream of celery soup

2 cans (5 ounces *each*) tuna in water, drained and flaked

1 cup water

2 carrots, chopped

1 small red onion, chopped

¼ teaspoon black pepper

1 raw egg, uncracked

8 ounces hot cooked egg noodles

Plain dry bread crumbs

2 tablespoons chopped fresh Italian parsley

1. Add soup, tuna, water, carrots, onion and pepper to **CROCK-POT**® slow cooker; stir to blend. Place whole unpeeled egg on top. Cover; cook on LOW 4 to 5 hours or on HIGH 1½ to 3 hours.

2. Remove egg to small bowl. Stir pasta into **CROCK-POT**® slow cooker. Cover; cook on HIGH 30 to 60 minutes or until onion is tender. Meanwhile, mash egg; mix in bread crumbs and parsley. Top casserole with bread crumb mixture.

NOTE: This casserole calls for a raw egg. The egg will hard-cook in its shell in the **CROCK-POT**® slow cooker.

MISO-POACHED SALMON

Makes 6 servings

1½ cups water

2 green onions, cut into 2-inch long pieces, plus additional for garnish

¼ cup yellow miso paste

¼ cup soy sauce

2 tablespoons sake

2 tablespoons mirin

1½ teaspoons grated fresh ginger

1 teaspoon minced garlic

6 (4 ounces *each*) salmon fillets

Hot cooked rice

1. Combine water, 2 green onions, miso paste, soy sauce, sake, mirin, ginger and garlic in **CROCK-POT**® slow cooker; stir to blend. Cover; cook on HIGH 30 minutes.

2. Turn **CROCK-POT**® slow cooker to LOW. Add salmon, skin side down. Cover; cook on LOW 30 to 60 minutes or until salmon turns opaque and flakes easily with fork. Serve over rice with cooking liquid as desired. Garnish with additional green onions.

CAJUN CHICKEN AND SHRIMP CREOLE

Makes 6 servings

1 pound skinless chicken thighs

1 red bell pepper, chopped

1 large onion, chopped

1 stalk celery, diced

1 can (about 15 ounces) diced tomatoes

1 clove garlic, minced

1 tablespoon sugar

1 teaspoon paprika

1 teaspoon Cajun seasoning

1 teaspoon salt

1 teaspoon black pepper

1 pound medium raw shrimp, peeled and deveined

1 tablespoon fresh lemon juice

Hot pepper sauce

1 cup hot cooked rice

1. Place chicken thighs in **CROCK-POT**® slow cooker. Add bell pepper, onion, celery, tomatoes, garlic, sugar, paprika, Cajun seasoning, salt and black pepper. Cover; cook on LOW 7 to 9 hours or on HIGH 3 to 4 hours.

2. Add shrimp, lemon juice and hot pepper sauce to **CROCK-POT**® slow cooker. Cover; cook on LOW 1 hour or on HIGH 30 minutes. Serve over rice.

TIP | Recipe can be doubled for a 5-, 6- or 7-quart **CROCK-POT**® slow cooker.

SEAFOOD AND TOMATO HERB RAGOÛT

Makes 6 to 8 servings

1 can (28 ounces) crushed tomatoes, undrained

1 can (8 ounces) tomato sauce

1 cup water

1 cup dry white wine

1 leek, chopped

1 green bell pepper, chopped

½ cup chopped celery

⅓ cup chopped fresh Italian parsley, plus additional for garnish

¼ cup extra virgin olive oil

3 cloves garlic, minced

2 tablespoons chopped fresh basil

1 tablespoon chopped fresh thyme

1 tablespoon chopped fresh oregano

1 teaspoon salt

½ teaspoon paprika

¼ teaspoon ground red pepper

1 pound orange roughy fillets or other white fish, such as cod or haddock, cubed

12 prawns, peeled and deveined

12 scallops, cleaned

1. Stir all ingredients except fish, prawns and scallops into **CROCK-POT**® slow cooker until well combined. Cover; cook on LOW 6 to 8 hours or on HIGH 3 to 4 hours.

2. Add fish, prawns and scallops to **CROCK-POT**® slow cooker. Cover; cook on HIGH 15 to 30 minutes or until seafood is just cooked through. Garnish with additional parsley.

COD TAPENADE

Makes 4 servings

4 cod fillets or other firm white fish (2 to 3 pounds *total*)
Salt and black pepper

2 lemons, thinly sliced
Tapenade (recipe follows)

1. Season cod with salt and pepper. Arrange half of lemon slices in bottom of **CROCK-POT**® slow cooker. Top with cod; cover with remaining lemon slices. Cover; cook on HIGH 1 hour or until fish is just cooked through. Prepare Tapenade.

2. Remove fish to serving plates; discard lemon. Top with Tapenade.

TAPENADE

Makes about 1 cup

½ pound pitted kalamata olives
2 tablespoons chopped fresh thyme or Italian parsley
2 tablespoons capers, drained
2 tablespoons anchovy paste

1 clove garlic
¼ teaspoon grated orange peel
⅛ teaspoon ground red pepper
½ cup olive oil

Place olives, thyme, capers, anchovy paste, garlic, orange peel and ground red pepper in food processor or blender; pulse to roughly chop. Add oil; pulse to form chunky paste.

TIP | In a hurry? Substitute store-brought tapenade for homemade!

SCALLOPS IN FRESH TOMATO AND HERB SAUCE

Makes 4 servings

2 tablespoons vegetable oil

1 medium red onion, peeled and diced

1 clove garlic, minced

3½ cups fresh tomatoes, peeled*

1 can (12 ounces) tomato pureé

1 can (6 ounces) tomato paste

¼ cup dry red wine

2 tablespoons chopped fresh Italian parsley

1 tablespoon chopped fresh oregano

¼ teaspoon black pepper

1½ pounds fresh scallops, cleaned and drained

Hot cooked pasta or rice (optional)

*To peel tomatoes, place one at a time in simmering water about 10 seconds. (Add 30 seconds if tomatoes are not fully ripened.) Immediately plunge into a bowl of cold water for another 10 seconds. Peel skin with a knife.

1. Heat oil in medium skillet over medium heat. Add onion and garlic; cook and stir 7 to 8 minutes or until onion is soft and translucent. Remove to **CROCK-POT**® slow cooker.

2. Add tomatoes, tomato purée, tomato paste, wine, parsley, oregano and pepper. Cover; cook on LOW 6 to 8 hours.

3. Turn **CROCK-POT**® slow cooker to HIGH. Add scallops. Cover; cook on HIGH 15 minutes or until scallops are cooked through. Serve over pasta, if desired.

VEGETARIAN

THAI RED CURRY WITH TOFU

Makes 4 servings

1 medium sweet potato, peeled and cut into 1-inch pieces

1 small eggplant, halved lengthwise and cut crosswise into ½-inch-wide halves

8 ounces extra firm tofu, cut into 1-inch pieces

½ cup green beans, cut into 1-inch pieces

½ red bell pepper, cut into ¼-inch-wide strips

2 tablespoons vegetable oil

5 medium shallots (about 1½ cups), thinly sliced

3 tablespoons Thai red curry paste

1 teaspoon minced garlic

1 teaspoon grated ginger

1 can (about 13 ounces) unsweetened coconut milk

1½ tablespoons soy sauce

1 tablespoon packed light brown sugar

¼ cup chopped fresh basil

2 tablespoons lime juice

Hot cooked rice (optional)

1. Coat inside of **CROCK-POT**® slow cooker with nonstick cooking spray. Add potato, eggplant, tofu, beans and bell pepper.

2. Heat oil in large skillet over medium heat. Add shallots; cook 5 minutes or until browned and tender. Add curry paste, garlic and ginger; cook and stir 1 minute. Add coconut milk, soy sauce and brown sugar; bring to a simmer. Pour mixture over vegetables in **CROCK-POT**® slow cooker.

3. Cover; cook on LOW 2 to 3 hours. Stir in basil and lime juice. Serve over rice, if desired.

SUMMER SQUASH LASAGNA

Makes 6 to 8 servings

3 tablespoons olive oil, divided

1 large onion, chopped

¼ teaspoon salt

2 cloves garlic, minced

2 medium zucchini (about 1 pound), cut lengthwise into ¼-inch strips

2 yellow squash (about 1 pound), cut lengthwise into ¼-inch strips

1 container (15 ounces) ricotta cheese

1 egg

¼ cup plus 2 tablespoons chopped fresh basil, divided

¼ teaspoon black pepper

½ cup grated Parmesan cheese, divided

1 jar (24 to 26 ounces) marinara sauce

12 uncooked whole wheat lasagna noodles

1 package (8 ounces) shredded mozzarella cheese, divided

1. Coat inside of **CROCK-POT®** slow cooker with nonstick cooking spray. Heat 1 tablespoon oil in large skillet over medium-high heat. Add onion and salt; cook and stir 5 minutes or until tender. Add garlic; cook and stir 1 minute. Remove to large bowl.

2. Heat 1 tablespoon oil in same skillet. Add zucchini; cook and stir 5 minutes or until lightly browned. Remove to bowl with onion. Repeat with remaining 1 tablespoon oil and squash.

3. Combine ricotta cheese, egg, ¼ cup basil, pepper and ¼ cup Parmesan cheese in medium bowl; stir to blend.

4. Prepare foil handles by using three 18×2-inch strips of heavy-duty foil or use regular foil folded to double thickness. Crisscross foil in spoke design; place across bottom and up side of **CROCK-POT®** slow cooker. Pour ½ cup marinara sauce evenly into bottom of **CROCK-POT®** slow cooker. Arrange 3 lasagna noodles in single layer (break to fit evenly); top with ⅔ cup ricotta mixture, ⅓ squash mixture, ¼ cup mozzarella and ½ cup marinara sauce. Repeat layers two times. Top with remaining 3 lasagna noodles, marinara sauce and mozzarella. Sprinkle with remaining ¼ cup Parmesan cheese.

5. Cover; cook on LOW 3 hours. Turn off heat. Uncover; let stand 30 minutes. Sprinkle with remaining 2 tablespoons basil before cutting and serving.

PESTO RICE AND BEANS

Makes 8 servings

1 can (about 15 ounces) Great Northern beans, rinsed and drained

1 can (about 14 ounces) vegetable broth

¾ cup uncooked converted long grain rice

1½ cups frozen cut green beans, thawed and drained

½ cup prepared pesto

Grated Parmesan cheese (optional)

1. Combine Great Northern beans, broth and rice in **CROCK-POT**® slow cooker; stir to blend. Cover; cook on LOW 2 hours.

2. Stir in green beans. Cover; cook on LOW 1 hour or until rice and beans are tender.

3. Turn off heat. Remove to **CROCK-POT**® stoneware to heatproof surface. Stir in pesto and cheese, if desired. Let stand, covered, 5 minutes or until cheese is melted. Serve immediately.

HOMESTYLE MAC 'N' CHEESE

Makes 6 to 8 servings

12 ounces uncooked elbow macaroni (about 3 cups)

2 cans (12 ounces *each*) evaporated milk

1 cup milk

⅓ cup all-purpose flour

¼ cup (½ stick) unsalted butter, melted

2 eggs, lightly beaten

1 teaspoon dry mustard

½ teaspoon salt

¼ teaspoon black pepper

4 cups (16 ounces) shredded sharp Cheddar cheese

Toasted plain dry bread crumbs (optional)

1. Coat inside of **CROCK-POT**® slow cooker with nonstick cooking spray. Bring large saucepan of lightly salted water to a boil. Add macaroni to saucepan; cook according to package directions. Drain. Remove to **CROCK-POT**® slow cooker.

2. Combine evaporated milk, milk, flour, butter, eggs, dry mustard, salt and pepper in large bowl; stir to blend. Pour into **CROCK-POT**® slow cooker. Stir in cheese until well combined. Cover; cook on LOW 3½ to 4 hours or until cheese is melted and macaroni is heated through. Stir well. Top each serving with bread crumbs, if desired.

ITALIAN EGGPLANT WITH MILLET AND PEPPER STUFFING

Makes 4 servings

¼ cup uncooked millet

2 small eggplants (about ¾ pound *total*), unpeeled

¼ cup chopped red bell pepper, divided

¼ cup chopped green bell pepper, divided

1 teaspoon olive oil

1 clove garlic, minced

1½ cups vegetable broth

½ teaspoon ground cumin

½ teaspoon dried oregano

⅛ teaspoon red pepper flakes

Sprigs fresh basil (optional)

1. Heat large skillet over medium heat. Add millet; cook and stir 5 minutes. Remove to small bowl; set aside. Cut eggplants lengthwise into halves. Scoop out flesh, leaving about ¼-inch-thick shell. Reserve shells; chop eggplant flesh. Combine 1 tablespoon red bell pepper and 1 tablespoon green bell pepper in small bowl; set aside.

2. Heat oil in same skillet over medium heat. Add chopped eggplant, remaining red and green bell peppers and garlic; cook and stir 8 minutes or until eggplant is tender.

3. Combine eggplant mixture, broth, millet, cumin, oregano and red pepper flakes in **CROCK-POT**® slow cooker. Cover; cook on LOW 4½ hours or until all liquid is absorbed.

4. Turn **CROCK-POT**® slow cooker to HIGH. Fill eggplant shells with eggplant-millet mixture. Sprinkle with reserved bell peppers. Place filled shells in **CROCK-POT**® slow cooker. Cover; cook on HIGH 1½ to 2 hours. Garnish with basil.

BLACK BEAN, ZUCCHINI AND CORN ENCHILADAS

Makes 6 servings

1 tablespoon vegetable oil

1 medium onion, chopped

2 medium zucchini

2 cups corn

1 large red bell pepper, chopped

1 teaspoon minced garlic

½ teaspoon salt

½ teaspoon ground cumin

¼ teaspoon ground coriander

1 can (about 14 ounces) black beans, rinsed and drained

2 jars (16 ounces *each*) salsa verde

12 (6-inch) corn tortillas

2½ cups (10 ounces) shredded Monterey Jack cheese

2 tablespoons chopped fresh cilantro

1. Heat oil in large skillet over medium heat. Add onion; cook 6 minutes or until softened. Add zucchini, corn and bell pepper; cook 2 minutes. Add garlic, salt, cumin and coriander; cook and stir 1 minute. Stir in beans. Remove from heat.

2. Prepare foil handles by using three 18×2-inch strips of heavy-duty foil or use regular foil folded to double thickness. Crisscross foil in spoke design; place across bottom and up side of **CROCK-POT**® slow cooker.

3. Pour 2 cups salsa in bottom of **CROCK-POT**® slow cooker. Arrange 3 tortillas in single layer, cutting the tortillas in half as needed to make them fit. Place 2 cups vegetable mixture over tortillas; sprinkle with ½ cup cheese. Repeat layering two more times. Layer with remaining 3 tortillas; top with 2 cups salsa. Sprinkle with remaining 1 cup cheese. Reserve remaining filling for another use.

4. Cover; cook on HIGH 2 hours or until cheese is bubbly and edges are lightly browned. Sprinkle with cilantro. Turn off heat. Let stand, uncovered, 10 minutes before removing from **CROCK-POT**® slow cooker using foil handles.

CHICKPEA AND VEGETABLE CURRY

Makes 4 servings

1 can (about 13 ounces) unsweetened coconut milk

1 cup vegetable broth, divided

2 teaspoons curry powder

¼ teaspoon ground red pepper

2 cups cut fresh green beans (1-inch pieces)

1 can (about 15 ounces) chickpeas, rinsed and drained

2 carrots, very thinly sliced

½ cup golden raisins

¼ cup all-purpose flour

2 cups hot cooked couscous

Chopped green onion and toasted sliced almonds (optional)

1. Coat inside of **CROCK-POT®** slow cooker with nonstick cooking spray. Combine coconut milk, ¾ cup broth, curry powder and ground red pepper in **CROCK-POT®** slow cooker. Stir in green beans, chickpeas, carrots and raisins. Cover; cook on LOW 6 to 7 hours or on HIGH 2½ to 3 hours or until vegetables are tender.

2. Stir remaining ¼ cup broth into flour in small bowl until smooth; whisk into vegetable mixture. Cover; cook on HIGH 15 minutes or until thickened. Ladle into shallow bowls; top with couscous, green onion and almonds, if desired.

SPINACH AND RICOTTA STUFFED SHELLS

Makes 6 servings

18 uncooked jumbo pasta shells (about half of a 12-ounce package)

1 package (15 ounces) ricotta cheese

7 ounces frozen chopped spinach, thawed and squeezed dry

½ cup grated Parmesan cheese

1 egg, lightly beaten

1 clove garlic, minced

½ teaspoon salt

1 jar (24 to 26 ounces) marinara sauce

½ cup (2 ounces) shredded mozzarella cheese

1 teaspoon olive oil

1. Cook pasta shells according to package directions until almost tender. Drain well. Combine ricotta cheese, spinach, Parmesan cheese, egg, garlic and salt in medium bowl.

2. Pour ¼ cup marinara sauce in bottom of **CROCK-POT**® slow cooker. Spoon 2 to 3 tablespoons ricotta mixture into 1 pasta shell and place in bottom of **CROCK-POT**® slow cooker. Repeat with enough additional shells to cover bottom of **CROCK-POT**® slow cooker. Top with another ¼ cup marinara sauce. Repeat with remaining pasta shells, ricotta mixture and marinara sauce. Top with mozzarella cheese. Drizzle with oil. Cover; cook on HIGH 3 to 4 hours or until mozzarella cheese is melted and sauce is heated through.

TOFU TIKKA MASALA

Makes 4 to 6 servings

1 package (14 to 16 ounces) extra firm tofu, cut into 1-inch pieces

½ cup whole milk yogurt

2 teaspoons salt, divided

1 tablespoon plus 1 teaspoon minced garlic, divided

2½ teaspoons grated fresh ginger, divided

2 tablespoons vegetable oil

1 medium onion, chopped

2 tablespoons tomato paste

1 tablespoon garam masala

1 teaspoon sugar

1 can (28 ounces) crushed tomatoes

½ cup whipping cream

3 tablespoons chopped fresh cilantro

Hot cooked basmati rice (optional)

1. Combine tofu, yogurt, 1 teaspoon salt, 1 teaspoon garlic and 1 teaspoon ginger in large bowl; stir to blend. Cover; refrigerate 1 hour or overnight.

2. Heat oil in large skillet over medium heat. Add onion; cook 8 minutes or until softened. Add remaining 1 tablespoon garlic, remaining 1½ teaspoons ginger, tomato paste, remaining 1 teaspoon salt and garam masala; cook and stir 1 minute. Add sugar and tomatoes; bring to a simmer. Remove onion mixture and tofu to **CROCK-POT**® slow cooker using slotted spoon; stir to blend.

3. Cover; cook on LOW 8 hours. Stir in cream and cilantro. Serve over rice, if desired.

BEAN AND VEGETABLE BURRITOS

Makes 4 servings

2 tablespoons chili powder

2 teaspoons dried oregano

1½ teaspoons ground cumin

1 sweet potato, diced

1 can (about 15 ounces) black beans, rinsed and drained

4 cloves garlic, minced

1 onion, halved and thinly sliced

1 jalapeño pepper, seeded and minced*

1 green bell pepper, chopped

1 cup frozen corn, thawed and drained

3 tablespoons lime juice

1 tablespoon chopped fresh cilantro

½ cup (3 ounces) shredded Monterey Jack cheese

4 (10-inch) flour tortillas, warmed

*Jalapeño peppers can sting and irritate the skin, so wear rubber gloves when handling peppers and do not touch your eyes.

1. Combine chili powder, oregano and cumin in small bowl.

2. Layer sweet potato, beans, half of chili powder mixture, garlic, onion, jalapeño pepper, bell pepper, remaining half of chili powder mixture and corn in **CROCK-POT**® slow cooker. Cover; cook on LOW 5 hours or until sweet potato is tender. Stir in lime juice and cilantro.

3. Spoon 2 tablespoons cheese down center of each tortilla. Top with 1 cup filling. Fold up bottom edges of tortillas over filling; fold in sides and roll to enclose filling.

VEGETARIAN LASAGNA

Makes 8 servings

1 eggplant, sliced into ½-inch rounds

½ teaspoon salt

3 tablespoons olive oil, divided

1 medium zucchini, thinly sliced

8 ounces mushrooms, sliced

1 small onion, diced

1 jar (24 to 26 ounces) pasta sauce

1 teaspoon dried basil

1 teaspoon dried oregano

1½ cups ricotta cheese

1½ cups (6 ounces) shredded mozzarella cheese

1 cup grated Parmesan cheese, divided

1 package (8 ounces) whole wheat lasagna noodles, cooked and drained

1. Sprinkle eggplant with salt; let stand 10 to 15 minutes. Rinse off excess salt and pat dry; brush with 1 tablespoon oil. Heat large skillet over medium heat. Add eggplant; cook 3 to 5 minutes or until browned on both sides. Remove to large paper towel-lined plate. Heat 1 tablespoon oil in same skillet over medium heat. Add zucchini; cook 3 to 5 minutes or until browned on both sides. Remove to separate large paper towel-lined plate.

2. Heat remaining 1 tablespoon oil in same skillet over medium heat; cook and stir mushrooms and onion until softened. Stir in pasta sauce, basil and oregano. Combine ricotta cheese, mozzarella cheese and ½ cup Parmesan cheese in medium bowl.

3. Spread one third of sauce mixture in bottom of **CROCK-POT**® slow cooker. Layer with one third lasagna noodles, half of eggplant and half of cheese mixture. Repeat layers. For last layer, use remaining one third of lasagna noodles, zucchini, remaining one third of sauce mixture and top with remaining ½ cup Parmesan cheese.

4. Cover; cook on LOW 6 hours. Turn off heat. Let stand 15 to 20 minutes before evenly cutting into eight squares.

BLACK BEAN STUFFED PEPPERS

Makes 6 servings

Nonstick cooking spray
1 medium onion, finely chopped
¼ teaspoon ground red pepper
¼ teaspoon dried oregano
¼ teaspoon ground cumin
¼ teaspoon chili powder
1 can (about 15 ounces) black beans, rinsed and drained

6 large green bell peppers, tops removed
1 cup (4 ounces) shredded Monterey Jack cheese
1 cup salsa
½ cup sour cream

1. Spray medium skillet with cooking spray; heat over medium heat. Add onion; cook and stir 3 to 5 minutes or until golden. Add ground red pepper, oregano, cumin and chili powder; cook and stir 1 minute.

2. Mash half of beans with onion mixture in medium bowl; stir in remaining half of beans. Spoon black bean mixture into bell peppers; sprinkle with cheese. Pour salsa over cheese. Place bell peppers in **CROCK-POT®** slow cooker.

3. Cover; cook on LOW 6 to 8 hours or on HIGH 3 to 4 hours. Serve with sour cream.

TIP | You may increase any of the recipe ingredients to taste except the salsa.

RATATOUILLE WITH CHICKPEAS

Makes 12 servings

3 tablespoons olive oil, divided

4 cloves garlic, minced

1 yellow onion, chopped

4 small Italian eggplants, peeled and chopped

1 red bell pepper, chopped

1 yellow bell pepper, chopped

1 orange bell pepper, chopped

3 small zucchini, chopped

1 can (about 15 ounces) chickpeas, rinsed and drained

2 cups canned crushed tomatoes

¼ cup chopped fresh basil

2 tablespoons chopped fresh thyme

½ to 1 teaspoon red pepper flakes

Sprigs fresh basil (optional)

1. Heat 1 tablespoon oil in large skillet over medium heat. Add garlic and onion; cook 2 to 3 minutes or until softened. Add eggplants; cook and stir 3 to 5 minutes. Cover; cook 4 to 5 minutes. Remove to **CROCK-POT®** slow cooker.

2. Add bell peppers, zucchini, chickpeas, tomatoes, chopped basil, thyme, remaining 2 tablespoons oil and red pepper flakes to **CROCK-POT®** slow cooker; stir to blend. Cover; cook on LOW 7 to 8 hours or on HIGH 4½ to 5 hours. Garnish with basil sprigs.

MANCHEGO EGGPLANT

Makes 12 servings

1 cup all-purpose flour

4 large eggplants, peeled and sliced horizontally into ¾-inch-thick pieces

2 tablespoons olive oil

1 jar (24 to 26 ounces) roasted garlic-flavor pasta sauce

2 tablespoons Italian seasoning

1 cup (4 ounces) grated manchego cheese

1 jar (24 to 26 ounces) roasted eggplant-flavor marinara pasta sauce

1. Place flour in medium shallow bowl. Add eggplants; toss to coat. Heat oil in large skillet over medium-high heat. Lightly brown eggplants in batches 3 to 4 minutes on each side.

2. Pour thin layer of garlic pasta sauce into bottom of **CROCK-POT**® slow cooker. Top with eggplant slices, Italian seasoning, cheese and marinara pasta sauce. Repeat layers until all ingredients have been used. Cover; cook on HIGH 2 hours.

CORN BREAD AND BEAN CASSEROLE

Makes 8 servings

- 1 medium onion, chopped
- 1 medium green bell pepper, diced
- 2 cloves garlic, minced
- 1 can (about 15 ounces) red kidney beans, rinsed and drained
- 1 can (about 15 ounces) pinto beans, rinsed and drained
- 1 can (about 15 ounces) diced tomatoes with mild green chiles
- 1 can (8 ounces) tomato sauce
- 1 teaspoon chili powder
- ½ teaspoon ground cumin
- ½ teaspoon black pepper
- ¼ teaspoon hot pepper sauce
- 1 cup yellow cornmeal
- 1 cup all-purpose flour
- 2½ teaspoons baking powder
- 1 tablespoon sugar
- ½ teaspoon salt
- 1¼ cups milk
- 2 eggs
- 3 tablespoons vegetable oil
- 1 can (8½ ounces) cream-style corn

1. Coat inside of **CROCK-POT®** slow cooker with nonstick cooking spray. Heat large skillet over medium heat. Add onion, bell pepper and garlic; cook and stir 5 minutes or until tender. Remove to **CROCK-POT®** slow cooker.

2. Add beans, diced tomatoes, tomato sauce, chili powder, cumin, black pepper and hot pepper sauce to **CROCK-POT®** slow cooker; stir to blend. Cover; cook on HIGH 1 hour.

3. Combine cornmeal, flour, baking powder, sugar and salt in large bowl; stir to blend. Stir in milk, eggs and oil; mix well. Stir in corn. Spoon evenly over bean mixture in **CROCK-POT®** slow cooker. Cover; cook on HIGH 1½ to 2 hours or until corn bread topping is golden brown.

TIP | Spoon any remaining corn bread topping into greased muffin cups. Bake 30 minutes at 375°F or until golden brown.

SIDES

CORN ON THE COB WITH GARLIC HERB BUTTER

Makes 4 to 5 servings

4 to 5 ears of corn, husked

½ cup (1 stick) unsalted butter, softened

3 to 4 cloves garlic, minced

2 tablespoons finely minced fresh Italian parsley

Salt and black pepper

1. Place each ear of corn on piece of foil. Combine butter, garlic and parsley in small bowl; spread onto corn. Season with salt and pepper; tightly seal foil.

2. Place in **CROCK-POT**® slow cooker, overlapping ears, if necessary. Add enough water to come one fourth of the way up each ear. Cover; cook on LOW 4 to 5 hours or on HIGH 2 to 2½ hours.

COLLARD GREENS

Makes 12 servings

1 tablespoon olive oil

3 turkey necks

5 bunches collard greens, stemmed and chopped

5 cups chicken broth

1 small onion, chopped

2 cloves garlic, minced

1 tablespoon cider vinegar

1 teaspoon sugar

Salt and black pepper

Red pepper flakes (optional)

1. Heat oil in large skillet over medium-high heat. Add turkey necks; cook and stir 3 to 5 minutes or until brown.

2. Combine turkey necks, collard greens, broth, onion and garlic in **CROCK-POT**® slow cooker; stir to blend. Cover; cook on LOW 5 to 6 hours. Remove and discard turkey necks. Stir in vinegar and sugar. Season with salt, black pepper and red pepper flakes, if desired.

MASHED ROOT VEGETABLES

Makes 6 servings

1 pound baking potatoes, peeled and cut into 1-inch pieces

1 pound turnips, peeled and cut into 1-inch pieces

12 ounces sweet potatoes, peeled and cut into 1-inch pieces

8 ounces parsnips, peeled and cut into ½-inch pieces

5 tablespoons butter

¼ cup water

2 teaspoons salt

¼ teaspoon black pepper

1 cup milk

1. Coat inside of **CROCK-POT**® slow cooker with nonstick cooking spray. Add baking potatoes, turnips, sweet potatoes, parsnips, butter, water, salt and pepper; stir to blend. Cover; cook on HIGH 3 to 4 hours.

2. Mash mixture with potato masher until smooth. Stir in milk. Cover; cook on HIGH 15 minutes.

CURRIED CAULIFLOWER AND POTATOES

Makes 6 servings

3 tablespoons vegetable oil

1 medium onion, chopped

1 tablespoon minced garlic

1 tablespoon curry powder

1½ teaspoons salt

1½ teaspoons grated fresh ginger

1 teaspoon ground turmeric

1 teaspoon yellow or brown mustard seeds

¼ teaspoon red pepper flakes

1 medium head cauliflower, cut into 1-inch pieces

2 pounds fingerling potatoes, cut into halves

½ cup water

1. Heat oil in medium skillet over medium heat. Add onion; cook 8 minutes or until softened. Add garlic, curry powder, salt, ginger, turmeric, mustard seeds and red pepper flakes; cook and stir 1 minute. Remove onion mixture to **CROCK-POT®** slow cooker.

2. Stir in cauliflower, potatoes and water. Cover; cook on HIGH 4 hours.

SIMMERED NAPA CABBAGE WITH DRIED APRICOTS

Makes 4 servings

4 cups napa cabbage or green cabbage, cored, cleaned and thinly sliced

1 cup chopped dried apricots

¼ cup honey

2 tablespoons orange juice

½ cup dry red wine

Salt and black pepper

Grated orange peel (optional)

1. Combine cabbage and apricots in **CROCK-POT**® slow cooker; toss to blend.

2. Combine honey and orange juice in small bowl; stir until smooth. Drizzle over cabbage. Add wine. Cover; cook on LOW 5 to 6 hours or on HIGH 2 to 3 hours.

3. Season with salt and pepper. Garnish with orange peel.

CHEESY POLENTA

Makes 6 servings

6 cups vegetable broth

1½ cups uncooked medium-grind instant polenta

½ cup grated Parmesan cheese, plus additional for serving

4 tablespoons (½ stick) unsalted butter, cubed

Fried sage leaves (optional)

1. Coat inside of **CROCK-POT**® slow cooker with nonstick cooking spray. Heat broth in large saucepan over high heat. Remove to **CROCK-POT**® slow cooker; whisk in polenta.

2. Cover; cook on LOW 2 to 2½ hours or until polenta is tender and creamy. Stir in ½ cup cheese and butter. Serve with additional cheese. Garnish with sage.

TIP | Spread any leftover polenta in a baking dish and refrigerate until cold. Cut cold polenta into sticks or slices. You can then fry or grill the polenta until lightly browned.

RED CABBAGE AND APPLES

Makes 6 servings

1 small head red cabbage, cored
   and thinly sliced
1 large apple, peeled and grated
¾ cup sugar

½ cup red wine vinegar
1 teaspoon ground cloves
   Fresh apple slices (optional)

Combine cabbage, grated apple, sugar, vinegar and cloves in **CROCK-POT**® slow cooker; stir to blend. Cover; cook on HIGH 6 hours, stirring halfway through cooking time. Garnish with apple slices.

CHEESY BROCCOLI CASSEROLE

Makes 4 to 6 servings

2 packages (10 ounces *each*)
   frozen chopped broccoli,
   thawed
1 can (10½ ounces) condensed
   cream of celery soup,
   undiluted
1¼ cups (5 ounces) shredded
   sharp Cheddar cheese,
   divided

¼ cup minced onion
1 teaspoon paprika
1 teaspoon hot pepper sauce
½ teaspoon celery seed
1 cup crushed potato chips or
   saltine crackers

1. Coat inside of **CROCK-POT**® slow cooker with nonstick cooking spray. Combine broccoli, soup, 1 cup cheese, onion, paprika, hot pepper sauce and celery seed in **CROCK-POT**® slow cooker; stir to blend. Cover; cook on LOW 5 to 6 hours or on HIGH 2½ to 3 hours.

2. Uncover; sprinkle top with potato chips and remaining ¼ cup cheese. Cook, uncovered, on HIGH 10 to 15 minutes or until cheese is melted.

VARIATIONS: Substitute thawed chopped spinach for the broccoli and top with spicy croutons.

RED CABBAGE AND APPLES

BBQ BAKED BEANS

Makes 12 servings

3 cans (about 15 ounces *each*)
   white beans, drained

4 slices bacon, chopped

¾ cup prepared barbecue sauce

½ cup maple syrup

1½ teaspoons ground mustard

Coat inside of **CROCK-POT**® slow cooker with nonstick cooking spray. Add beans, bacon, barbecue sauce, syrup and mustard; stir to blend. Cover; cook on LOW 4 hours, stirring halfway through cooking time.

FIVE-INGREDIENT MUSHROOM STUFFING

Makes 12 servings

6 tablespoons (¾ stick) unsalted butter

2 medium onions, chopped

1 pound sliced white mushrooms

¼ teaspoon salt

5 cups bagged stuffing mix, any seasoning

1 cup vegetable broth

Chopped fresh Italian parsley (optional)

1. Melt butter in large skillet over medium-high heat. Add onions, mushrooms and salt; cook and stir 20 minutes or until vegetables are browned and most liquid is absorbed. Remove onion mixture to **CROCK-POT**® slow cooker.

2. Stir in stuffing mix and broth. Cover; cook on LOW 3 hours. Garnish with parsley.

LEMON CAULIFLOWER

Makes 6 servings

1 tablespoon butter

3 cloves garlic, minced

2 tablespoons lemon juice

½ cup water

4 tablespoons chopped fresh Italian parsley, divided

½ teaspoon grated lemon peel

6 cups (about 1½ pounds) cauliflower florets

¼ cup grated Parmesan cheese

Lemon slices (optional)

1. Heat butter in small saucepan over medium heat. Add garlic; cook and stir 2 to 3 minutes or until soft. Stir in lemon juice and water.

2. Combine garlic mixture, 1 tablespoon parsley, lemon peel and cauliflower in **CROCK-POT**® slow cooker; stir to blend. Cover; cook on LOW 4 hours.

3. Sprinkle with remaining 3 tablespoons parsley and cheese before serving. Garnish with lemon slices.

CHEESY MASHED POTATO CASSEROLE

Makes 10 to 12 servings

4 pounds Yukon Gold potatoes, cut into 1-inch pieces

2 cups vegetable broth

3 tablespoons unsalted butter, cubed

½ cup milk, heated

⅓ cup sour cream

2 cups (8 ounces) shredded sharp Cheddar cheese, plus additional for garnish

½ teaspoon salt

¼ teaspoon black pepper

Chopped fresh Italian parsley (optional)

1. Coat inside of **CROCK-POT**® slow cooker with nonstick cooking spray. Add potatoes and broth; dot with butter. Cover; cook on LOW 4½ to 5 hours.

2. Mash potatoes with potato masher; stir in milk, sour cream, 2 cups cheese, salt and pepper until cheese is melted. Garnish with additional cheese and parsley.

LEMON CAULIFLOWER

LEMON AND TANGERINE GLAZED CARROTS

Makes 10 to 12 servings

6 cups sliced carrots

1½ cups apple juice

6 tablespoons (¾ stick) butter

¼ cup packed brown sugar

2 tablespoons grated lemon peel

2 tablespoons grated tangerine peel

½ teaspoon salt

Chopped fresh Italian parsley (optional)

Combine carrots, apple juice, butter, brown sugar, lemon peel, tangerine peel and salt in **CROCK-POT**® slow cooker; stir to blend. Cover; cook on LOW 4 to 5 hours or on HIGH 1 to 3 hours. Garnish with parsley.

PARMESAN POTATO WEDGES

Makes 6 servings

---

2 pounds red potatoes, cut into ½-inch wedges

¼ cup finely chopped yellow onion

1½ teaspoons dried oregano

½ teaspoon salt

¼ teaspoon black pepper

2 tablespoons butter, cubed

¼ cup grated Parmesan cheese

Layer potatoes, onion, oregano, salt and pepper in **CROCK-POT**® slow cooker; dot with butter. Cover; cook on HIGH 4 hours. Remove potatoes to large serving platter; sprinkle with cheese.

WILD RICE AND MUSHROOM CASSEROLE

Makes 4 to 6 servings

2 tablespoons olive oil

1 large green bell pepper, finely diced

8 ounces mushrooms, thinly sliced

½ medium red onion, finely diced

2 cloves garlic, minced

1 can (14 ounces) diced tomatoes, drained

1 teaspoon dried oregano

1 teaspoon paprika

2 tablespoons butter

2 tablespoons all-purpose flour

1½ cups milk

2 cups (8 ounces) shredded pepper jack, Cheddar or Swiss cheese

1 teaspoon salt

½ teaspoon black pepper

2 cups wild rice, cooked according to package directions

Sprigs fresh oregano (optional)

1. Coat inside of **CROCK-POT®** slow cooker with nonstick cooking spray. Heat oil in large skillet over medium heat. Add bell pepper, mushrooms and onion; cook 5 to 6 minutes stirring occasionally, until vegetables soften. Add garlic, tomatoes, dried oregano and paprika; cook 3 to 5 minutes or until heated through. Remove to large bowl to cool.

2. Melt butter in same skillet over medium heat; whisk in flour. Cook and stir 4 to 5 minutes or until smooth and golden. Whisk in milk; bring to a boil. Whisk in cheese. Season with salt and black pepper.

3. Combine wild rice with vegetables in large bowl. Fold in cheese sauce; mix gently. Pour wild rice mixture into **CROCK-POT®** slow cooker. Cover; cook on LOW 4 to 6 hours or on HIGH 2 to 3 hours. Garnish with fresh oregano.

SWEET POTATO AND PECAN CASSEROLE

Makes 6 to 8 servings

1 can (40 ounces) sweet
  potatoes, drained and mashed

½ cup apple juice

⅓ cup plus 2 tablespoons butter,
  melted and divided

½ teaspoon salt

½ teaspoon ground cinnamon

¼ teaspoon black pepper

2 eggs, beaten

⅓ cup chopped pecans

⅓ cup packed brown sugar

2 tablespoons all-purpose flour

1. Combine potatoes, apple juice, ⅓ cup butter, salt, cinnamon and pepper in large bowl; beat in eggs. Pour mixture into **CROCK-POT**® slow cooker.

2. Combine pecans, brown sugar, flour and remaining 2 tablespoons butter in small bowl; stir to blend. Spread over sweet potatoes. Cover; cook on HIGH 3 to 4 hours.

ASPARAGUS AND CHEESE

Makes 4 to 6 servings

1½ pounds fresh asparagus, trimmed

2 cups crushed saltine crackers

1 can (10¾ ounces) condensed cream of asparagus soup, undiluted

1 can (10¾ ounces) condensed cream of chicken or cream of celery soup, undiluted

⅔ cup silvered almonds

4 ounces American cheese, cubed

1 egg

Combine asparagus, crackers, soups, almonds, cheese and egg in **CROCK-POT®** slow cooker; toss to coat. Cover; cook on HIGH 3 to 3½ hours.

TIP | Cooking times are guidelines. **CROCK-POT®** slow cookers, just like ovens, cook differently depending on a variety of factors. For example, cooking times will be longer at higher altitudes. You may need to slightly adjust cooking times.

MASHED RUTABAGAS AND POTATOES

Makes 8 servings

2 pounds rutabagas, peeled and cut into ½-inch pieces

1 pound potatoes, peeled and cut into ½-inch pieces

½ cup milk

½ teaspoon ground nutmeg

2 tablespoons chopped fresh Italian parsley

Sprigs fresh Italian parsley (optional)

1. Place rutabagas and potatoes in **CROCK-POT®** slow cooker; add enough water to cover vegetables. Cover; cook on LOW 6 hours or on HIGH 3 hours. Remove vegetables to large bowl using slotted spoon. Discard cooking liquid.

2. Mash vegetables with potato masher. Add milk, nutmeg and chopped parsley; stir until smooth. Garnish with parsley sprigs.

GREEN BEAN CASSEROLE

Makes 6 servings

2 packages (10 ounces *each*) frozen green beans

1 can (10¾ ounces) condensed cream of mushroom soup, undiluted

1 tablespoon chopped fresh Italian parsley

1 tablespoon chopped roasted red peppers

1 teaspoon dried sage

½ teaspoon salt

½ teaspoon black pepper

¼ teaspoon ground nutmeg

½ cup toasted slivered almonds*

To toast almonds, spread in single layer in small heavy skillet. Cook and stir over medium heat 1 to 2 minutes or until nuts are lightly browned.

Combine beans, soup, parsley, red peppers, sage, salt, black pepper and nutmeg in **CROCK-POT®** slow cooker; stir to blend. Cover; cook on LOW 3 to 4 hours. Sprinkle with almonds.

MASHED RUTABAGAS AND POTATOES

DELUXE POTATO CASSEROLE

Makes 8 to 10 servings

1 can (10¾ ounces) condensed cream of chicken soup, undiluted

1 container (8 ounces) sour cream

¼ cup chopped onion

¼ cup (½ stick) plus 3 tablespoons melted butter, divided

1 teaspoon salt

2 pounds red potatoes, peeled and diced

2 cups (8 ounces) shredded Cheddar cheese

1½ to 2 cups stuffing mix

1. Combine soup, sour cream, onion, ¼ cup butter and salt in small bowl; stir to blend.

2. Combine potatoes and cheese in **CROCK-POT®** slow cooker. Pour soup mixture over potato mixture; mix well. Sprinkle stuffing mix over potato mixture; drizzle with remaining 3 tablespoons butter. Cover; cook on LOW 8 to 10 hours or on HIGH 5 to 6 hours.

SLOW-COOKED SUCCOTASH

Makes 8 servings

---

2 teaspoons olive oil

1 cup diced onion

1 cup diced green bell pepper

1 cup diced celery

1 teaspoon paprika

1½ cups frozen corn

1½ cups frozen lima beans

1 cup canned diced tomatoes

2 teaspoons dried parsley flakes *or* 1 tablespoon minced fresh Italian parsley

Salt and black pepper

1. Heat oil in large skillet over medium heat. Add onion, bell pepper and celery; cook and stir 5 minutes or until vegetables are crisp-tender. Stir in paprika.

2. Add onion mixture, corn, beans, tomatoes and parsley flakes to **CROCK-POT**® slow cooker. Season with salt and black pepper; stir to blend. Cover; cook on LOW 6 to 8 hours or on HIGH 3 to 4 hours.

DESSERTS AND DRINKS

ROCKY ROAD BROWNIE BOTTOMS

Makes 6 servings

½ cup packed brown sugar

½ cup water

2 tablespoons unsweetened cocoa powder

2½ cups packaged brownie mix

1 package (about 4 ounces) instant chocolate pudding mix

½ cup milk chocolate chips

2 eggs, beaten

3 tablespoons butter, melted

2 cups mini marshmallows

1 cup chopped pecans or walnuts, toasted*

½ cup chocolate syrup

To toast pecans, cook and stir in small skillet over medium-low heat about 5 minutes or until lightly browned.

1. Prepare foil handles by tearing off three 18×2-inch strips heavy foil (or use regular foil folded to double thickness). Crisscross foil strips in spoke design; place in **CROCK-POT**® slow cooker. Coat inside of **CROCK-POT**® slow cooker with nonstick cooking spray.

2. Combine brown sugar, water and cocoa in small saucepan over medium heat; bring to a boil over medium-high heat. Meanwhile, combine brownie mix, pudding mix, chocolate chips, eggs and butter in medium bowl; stir until well blended. Spread batter in **CROCK-POT**® slow cooker; pour boiling sugar mixture over batter.

3. Cover; cook on HIGH 1½ hours. Turn off heat. Top brownies with marshmallows, pecans and chocolate syrup. Let stand 15 minutes. Use foil handles to lift brownie to serving platter.

NOTE: Recipe can be doubled for a 5-, 6- or 7-quart **CROCK-POT**® slow cooker.

BANANAS FOSTER

Makes 12 servings

- 12 bananas, cut into quarters
- 1 cup flaked coconut
- 1 cup dark corn syrup
- ⅔ cup butter, melted
- ¼ cup lemon juice
- 2 teaspoons grated lemon peel
- 2 teaspoons rum
- 1 teaspoon ground cinnamon
- ½ teaspoon salt
- 12 slices pound cake
- 1 quart vanilla ice cream

1. Combine bananas and coconut in **CROCK-POT**® slow cooker. Combine corn syrup, butter, lemon juice, lemon peel, rum, cinnamon and salt in medium bowl; stir to blend. Pour over bananas.

2. Cover; cook on LOW 1 to 2 hours. To serve, arrange bananas on pound cake slices. Top with ice cream and warm sauce.

HOT MULLED CIDER

Makes 16 servings

- ½ gallon apple cider
- ½ cup packed brown sugar
- 1½ teaspoons balsamic or cider vinegar (optional)
- 1 teaspoon vanilla
- 1 whole cinnamon stick
- 6 whole cloves
- ½ cup applejack or bourbon (optional)

1. Combine cider, brown sugar, vinegar, if desired, vanilla, cinnamon stick and cloves in **CROCK-POT**® slow cooker; stir to blend. Cover; cook on LOW 5 to 6 hours.

2. Remove and discard cinnamon stick and cloves. Stir in applejack just before serving, if desired. Serve warm in mugs.

BANANAS FOSTER

MINTED HOT COCOA

Makes 6 to 8 servings

6 **cups milk**

¾ **cup semisweet chocolate pieces**

½ **cup sugar**

½ **cup unsweetened cocoa powder**

1 **teaspoon vanilla**

½ **teaspoon mint extract**

10 **sprigs fresh mint, tied together with kitchen string, plus additional for garnish**

Whipped cream (optional)

1. Add milk, chocolate, sugar, cocoa, vanilla and mint extract to **CROCK-POT®** slow cooker; stir to blend. Add 10 mint sprigs. Cover; cook on LOW 3 to 4 hours.

2. Remove and discard mint sprigs. Whisk cocoa mixture well. Cover until ready to serve. Garnish each serving with whipped cream and additional mint sprigs.

GINGER PEAR CIDER

Makes 8 to 10 servings

8 cups pear juice or cider
¾ cup lemon juice
¼ to ½ cup honey
10 whole cloves

2 whole cinnamon sticks, plus
additional for garnish
8 slices fresh ginger

1. Combine pear juice, lemon juice, honey, cloves, 2 cinnamon sticks and ginger in 5-quart **CROCK-POT®** slow cooker.

2. Cover; cook on LOW 5 to 6 hours or on HIGH 2½ to 3 hours. Remove and discard cloves, cinnamon sticks and ginger before serving. Garnish with additional cinnamon sticks.

PLUM BREAD PUDDING

Makes 12 to 16 servings

---

1 loaf (1 pound) sliced egg bread, lightly toasted*

2 tablespoons unsalted butter, divided

12 large unpeeled Italian plums, pitted and cut into wedges (about 4 cups *total*), divided

1½ cups plus 2 tablespoons sugar, divided

3 cups half-and-half

10 eggs

1¼ cups milk

2 teaspoons vanilla

¾ teaspoon salt

¾ teaspoon ground cinnamon

Sweetened whipped cream or vanilla ice cream (optional)

Use an egg-rich bread, such as challah, for best results. For a more delicate bread pudding, substitute cinnamon rolls or plain Danish rolls.

1. Coat inside of 6-quart **CROCK-POT**® slow cooker with nonstick cooking spray. Cut toasted bread into 1-inch cubes; set aside.

2. Melt 1 tablespoon butter in large skillet over medium-high heat. Add half of sliced plums and 1 tablespoon sugar; cook 2 minutes or until plums are pulpy and release their juices. Pour plums and juices into medium bowl; repeat with remaining 1 tablespoon butter, remaining plums and 1 tablespoon sugar. Set aside.

3. Add half-and-half, eggs, remaining 1½ cups sugar, milk, vanilla, salt and cinnamon in large bowl; stir in bread, plums and any accumulated juices. Spoon into **CROCK-POT**® slow cooker. Cover; cook on HIGH 3 hours or until pudding is firm when gently shaken and thin knife inserted halfway between center and edge comes out clean. Remove stoneware from base; cool 15 minutes. Serve with whipped cream, if desired.

PEACH BREAD PUDDING: If fresh plums are not available, substitute 9 large peaches, peeled, pitted and cut into wedges or 4 cups frozen sliced peaches, thawed (juices reserved).

FUDGE AND CREAM PUDDING CAKE

Makes 8 to 10 servings

2 tablespoons unsalted butter, melted

1 cup all-purpose flour

½ cup packed light brown sugar

5 tablespoons unsweetened cocoa powder, divided

2 teaspoons baking powder

½ teaspoon ground cinnamon

⅛ teaspoon salt

1 cup cream

1 tablespoon vegetable oil

1 teaspoon vanilla

1½ cups hot water

½ cup packed dark brown sugar

Whipped cream (optional)

1. Prepare foil handles by tearing off three 18×2-inch strips heavy foil (or use regular foil folded to double thickness). Crisscross foil strips in spoke design; place in **CROCK-POT**® slow cooker. Coat inside of 5-quart **CROCK-POT**® slow cooker with melted butter.

2. Combine flour, light brown sugar, 3 tablespoons cocoa, baking powder, cinnamon and salt in medium bowl; stir to blend. Combine cream, oil and vanilla in small bowl. Add cream mixture to flour mixture; stir to blend. Pour batter into **CROCK-POT**® slow cooker.

3. Combine hot water, dark brown sugar and remaining 2 tablespoons cocoa in medium bowl; stir well. Pour sauce over cake batter. *Do not stir.* Cover; cook on HIGH 2 hours. Turn off heat. Let stand 10 minutes. Remove with foil handles to wire rack. Cut into wedges to serve. Serve with whipped cream, if desired.

PEACH COBBLER

Makes 4 to 6 servings

2 packages (16 ounces *each*) frozen peaches, thawed and drained

½ cup plus 1 tablespoon sugar, divided

2 teaspoons ground cinnamon, divided

½ teaspoon ground nutmeg

¾ cup all-purpose flour

6 tablespoons (¾ stick) butter, cubed

Whipped cream (optional)

1. Coat inside of **CROCK-POT®** slow cooker with nonstick cooking spray. Combine peaches, ½ cup sugar, 1½ teaspoons cinnamon and nutmeg in **CROCK-POT®** slow cooker; stir to blend.

2. Combine flour, remaining 1 tablespoon sugar and remaining ½ teaspoon cinnamon in small bowl. Cut in butter with pastry blender or two knives until mixture resembles coarse crumbs. Sprinkle over peach mixture. Cover; cook on HIGH 2 hours. Serve with whipped cream, if desired.

WARM PEANUT-CARAMEL DIP

Makes 1¾ cups

¾ cup peanut butter

¾ cup caramel ice cream topping

⅓ cup milk

1 apple, thinly sliced

4 large pretzel rods, cut in half

1. Add peanut butter, caramel topping and milk to medium saucepan; cook and stir 3 to 5 minutes over medium heat until smooth and creamy.

2. Coat inside of **CROCK-POT®** slow cooker with nonstick cooking spray. Fill with warm dip. Serve with apple slices and pretzels.

PEACH COBBLER

BRIOCHE AND AMBER RUM CUSTARD

Makes 4 to 6 servings

2 tablespoons unsalted butter, melted

3½ cups whipping cream

4 eggs

½ cup packed dark brown sugar

⅓ cup amber or light rum

2 teaspoons vanilla

1 loaf (20 to 22 ounces) brioche bread, torn into pieces *or* 5 large brioche, cut into thirds*

½ cup coarsely chopped pecans

Caramel or butterscotch ice cream topping (optional)

If desired, trim and discard heels.

1. Coat inside of **CROCK-POT**® slow cooker with melted butter. Combine cream, eggs, brown sugar, rum and vanilla in large bowl; stir well.

2. Mound one fourth of brioche pieces in bottom of **CROCK-POT**® slow cooker. Ladle one fourth of cream mixture over brioche. Sprinkle with one third of pecans. Repeat layers with remaining brioche, cream mixture and pecans until all ingredients are used.

3. Cover; cook on LOW 3 to 3½ hours or on HIGH 1½ to 2 hours or until custard is set and toothpick inserted into center comes out clean.

4. Drizzle with caramel topping, if desired. Serve warm.

CINNAMON LATTÉ

Makes 6 to 8 servings

6 cups double-strength brewed coffee*

2 cups half-and-half

1 cup sugar

1 teaspoon vanilla

3 whole cinnamon sticks, plus additional for garnish

Whipped cream (optional)

Double the amount of coffee grounds normally used to brew coffee. Or substitute 8 teaspoons instant coffee dissolved in 6 cups boiling water.

1. Add coffee, half-and-half, sugar and vanilla to **CROCK-POT®** slow cooker; stir to blend. Add 3 cinnamon sticks. Cover; cook on HIGH 3 hours.

2. Remove and discard cinnamon sticks. Serve latté in tall coffee mugs. Garnish with additional cinnamon sticks and whipped cream.

CHAI TEA

Makes 8 to 10 servings

2 quarts (8 cups) water

8 bags black tea

¾ cup sugar*

8 slices fresh ginger

5 whole cinnamon sticks, plus additional for garnish

16 whole cloves

16 whole cardamom seeds, pods removed (optional)

1 cup milk

Chai tea is typically sweet. For less-sweet tea, reduce sugar to ½ cup.

1. Combine water, tea bags, sugar, ginger, 5 cinnamon sticks, cloves and cardamom, if desired, in **CROCK-POT®** slow cooker; stir to blend. Cover; cook on HIGH 2 to 2½ hours.

2. Strain mixture; discard solids. (At this point, tea may be covered and refrigerated up to 3 days.)

3. Stir in milk just before serving. Garnish with additional cinnamon sticks.

CINNAMON LATTÉ

MIXED BERRY COBBLER

Makes 8 servings

- 1 package (16 ounces) frozen mixed berries
- ½ cup granulated sugar
- 2 tablespoons quick-cooking tapioca
- 2 teaspoons grated lemon peel
- 1½ cups all-purpose flour
- ½ cup packed light brown sugar
- 2¼ teaspoons baking powder
- ¼ teaspoon ground nutmeg
- ½ cup milk
- ⅓ cup butter, melted
- Vanilla ice cream (optional)

1. Coat inside of **CROCK-POT**® slow cooker with nonstick cooking spray. Stir berries, granulated sugar, tapioca and lemon peel in medium bowl. Remove to **CROCK-POT**® slow cooker.

2. Combine flour, brown sugar, baking powder and nutmeg in medium bowl. Add milk and butter; stir just until blended. Drop spoonfuls of dough on top of berry mixture. Cover; cook on LOW 4 hours. Turn off heat. Uncover; let stand 30 minutes. Serve with ice cream, if desired.

TIP | Cobblers are year-round favorites. Experiment with seasonal fresh fruits, such as pears, plums, peaches, rhubarb, blueberries, raspberries, strawberries, blackberries or gooseberries.

TEQUILA-POACHED PEARS

Makes 4 servings

4 Anjou pears, peeled
2 cups water
1 can (11½ ounces) pear nectar

1 cup tequila
½ cup sugar
Grated peel and juice of 1 lime

1. Place pears in **CROCK-POT**® slow cooker. Combine water, nectar, tequila, sugar, lime peel and lime juice in medium saucepan. Bring to a boil over medium-high heat, stirring frequently. Boil 1 minute; pour over pears.

2. Cover; cook on LOW 4 to 6 hours or on HIGH 2 to 3 hours or until pears are tender. Serve warm with poaching liquid.

TIP | Poaching fruit in a sugar, juice or alcohol syrup helps the fruit retain its shape and become more flavorful.

TRIPLE CHOCOLATE FANTASY

Makes 36 pieces

2 pounds white almond bark, broken into pieces

1 bar (4 ounces) sweetened chocolate, broken into pieces*

1 package (12 ounces) semisweet chocolate chips

2 cups coarsely chopped pecans, toasted**

*Use your favorite high-quality chocolate candy bar.

**To toast pecans, spread in single layer in heavy skillet. Cook and stir over medium heat 1 to 2 minutes or until nuts are lightly browned.

1. Line mini muffin pan with paper baking cups. Place bark, sweetened chocolate and chocolate chips in **CROCK-POT**® slow cooker. Cover; cook on HIGH 1 hour. *Do not stir.*

2. Turn **CROCK-POT**® slow cooker to LOW. Cover; cook on LOW 1 hour, stirring every 15 minutes. Stir in pecans.

3. Drop mixture by tablespoonfuls into prepared baking cups; cool completely. Store in tightly covered container.

VARIATIONS: Here are a few ideas for other imaginative items to add in along with or instead of the pecans: raisins, crushed peppermint candy, candy-coated baking bits, crushed toffee, peanuts or pistachio nuts, chopped gum drops, chopped dried fruit, candied cherries, chopped marshmallows and/or sweetened coconut.

STRAWBERRY RHUBARB CRISP

Makes 8 servings

4 cups sliced hulled fresh strawberries

4 cups diced rhubarb (about 5 stalks), cut into ½-inch dice

1½ cups granulated sugar

2 tablespoons lemon juice

2 tablespoons water

1½ tablespoons cornstarch

1 cup all-purpose flour

1 cup old-fashioned oats

½ cup granulated sugar

½ cup packed brown sugar

½ teaspoon ground ginger

½ teaspoon ground nutmeg

½ cup (1 stick) butter, cubed

½ cup sliced almonds, toasted*

*To toast almonds, spread in single layer in heavy skillet. Cook over medium heat 1 to 2 minutes or until nuts are lightly browned, stirring frequently.

1. Coat inside of **CROCK-POT®** slow cooker with nonstick cooking spray. Place strawberries, rhubarb, granulated sugar and lemon juice in **CROCK-POT®** slow cooker; stir to blend. Cover; cook on HIGH 1½ hours or until fruit is tender.

2. Stir water into cornstarch in small bowl until smooth; whisk into **CROCK-POT®** slow cooker. Cover; cook on HIGH 15 minutes or until thickened.

3. Preheat oven to 375°F. Combine flour, oats, sugars, ginger and nutmeg in medium bowl. Cut in butter using pastry blender or two knives until mixture resembles coarse crumbs. Stir in almonds.

4. Remove lid from **CROCK-POT®** slow cooker and gently sprinkle topping onto fruit. Remove stoneware to oven. Bake 15 to 20 minutes or until topping begins to brown.

FRUIT AND NUT BAKED APPLES

Makes 4 servings

4 large baking apples, such as Rome Beauty or Jonathan

1 tablespoon lemon juice

⅓ cup chopped dried apricots

⅓ cup chopped walnuts or pecans

3 tablespoons packed brown sugar

½ teaspoon ground cinnamon

2 tablespoons unsalted butter, melted

½ cup water

Caramel ice cream topping (optional)

1. Scoop out center of each apple, leaving 1½-inch-wide cavity about ½ inch from bottom. Peel top of apple down about 1 inch. Brush peeled edges evenly with lemon juice. Combine apricots, walnuts, brown sugar and cinnamon in small bowl; stir to blend. Add butter; mix well. Spoon mixture evenly into apple cavities.

2. Pour water in bottom of **CROCK-POT**® slow cooker. Place 2 apples in bottom of **CROCK-POT**® slow cooker. Arrange remaining 2 apples above but not directly on top of bottom apples. Cover; cook on LOW 3 to 4 hours or until apples are tender. Serve warm or at room temperature with caramel ice cream topping, if desired.

TIP | Ever wonder why you need to brush lemon juice around the top of an apple? Citrus fruits, like lemons, contain an acid that keeps apples, potatoes and other white vegetables from discoloring once they are cut or peeled.

CHERRY DELIGHT

Makes 8 to 10 servings

1 can (21 ounces) cherry pie filling

1 package (about 18 ounces) yellow cake mix

½ cup (1 stick) butter, melted

⅓ cup chopped walnuts

Place pie filling in **CROCK-POT®** slow cooker. Combine cake mix and butter in medium bowl; stir to blend. Spread evenly over pie filling. Sprinkle with walnuts. Cover; cook on LOW 3 to 4 hours or on HIGH 1½ to 2 hours.

APPLE-PECAN BREAD PUDDING

Makes 8 servings

8 cups bread, cubed

3 cups Granny Smith apples, cubed

1 cup chopped pecans

8 eggs

1 can (12 ounces) evaporated milk

1 cup packed brown sugar

½ cup apple cider or apple juice

2 teaspoons ground cinnamon

1 teaspoon ground nutmeg

1 teaspoon vanilla

½ teaspoon salt

½ teaspoon ground allspice

Ice cream (optional)

Caramel ice cream topping (optional)

1. Coat inside of **CROCK-POT**® slow cooker with nonstick cooking spray. Add bread cubes, apples and pecans.

2. Combine eggs, evaporated milk, brown sugar, apple cider, cinnamon, nutmeg, vanilla, salt and allspice in large bowl; whisk to blend. Pour egg mixture into **CROCK-POT**® slow cooker. Cover; cook on LOW 3 hours. Serve with ice cream topped with caramel ice cream topping, if desired.

INDEX

METRIC CONVERSION CHART

VOLUME MEASUREMENTS (dry)

$1/8$ teaspoon = 0.5 mL
$1/4$ teaspoon = 1 mL
$1/2$ teaspoon = 2 mL
$3/4$ teaspoon = 4 mL
1 teaspoon = 5 mL
1 tablespoon = 15 mL
2 tablespoons = 30 mL
$1/4$ cup = 60 mL
$1/3$ cup = 75 mL
$1/2$ cup = 125 mL
$2/3$ cup = 150 mL
$3/4$ cup = 175 mL
1 cup = 250 mL
2 cups = 1 pint = 500 mL
3 cups = 750 mL
4 cups = 1 quart = 1 L

VOLUME MEASUREMENTS (fluid)

1 fluid ounce (2 tablespoons) = 30 mL
4 fluid ounces ($1/2$ cup) = 125 mL
8 fluid ounces (1 cup) = 250 mL
12 fluid ounces ($1 1/2$ cups) = 375 mL
16 fluid ounces (2 cups) = 500 mL

WEIGHTS (mass)

$1/2$ ounce = 15 g
1 ounce = 30 g
3 ounces = 90 g
4 ounces = 120 g
8 ounces = 225 g
10 ounces = 285 g
12 ounces = 360 g
16 ounces = 1 pound = 450 g

DIMENSIONS

$1/16$ inch = 2 mm
$1/8$ inch = 3 mm
$1/4$ inch = 6 mm
$1/2$ inch = 1.5 cm
$3/4$ inch = 2 cm
1 inch = 2.5 cm

OVEN TEMPERATURES

250°F = 120°C
275°F = 140°C
300°F = 150°C
325°F = 160°C
350°F = 180°C
375°F = 190°C
400°F = 200°C
425°F = 220°C
450°F = 230°C

BAKING PAN SIZES

Utensil	Size in Inches/Quarts	Metric Volume	Size in Centimeters
Baking or Cake Pan (square or rectangular)	$8 \times 8 \times 2$	2 L	$20 \times 20 \times 5$
	$9 \times 9 \times 2$	2.5 L	$23 \times 23 \times 5$
	$12 \times 8 \times 2$	3 L	$30 \times 20 \times 5$
	$13 \times 9 \times 2$	3.5 L	$33 \times 23 \times 5$
Loaf Pan	$8 \times 4 \times 3$	1.5 L	$20 \times 10 \times 7$
	$9 \times 5 \times 3$	2 L	$23 \times 13 \times 7$
Round Layer Cake Pan	$8 \times 1 1/2$	1.2 L	20×4
	$9 \times 1 1/2$	1.5 L	23×4
Pie Plate	$8 \times 1 1/4$	750 mL	20×3
	$9 \times 1 1/4$	1 L	23×3
Baking Dish or Casserole	1 quart	1 L	—
	$1 1/2$ quart	1.5 L	—
	2 quart	2 L	—